Sheltering
with the Psalms:
30 Days of Prayer
with Charles Wesley

Paul W. Chilcote

ALDERSGATE
PRESS

Cleveland, TN

Published in the United States of America

By Aldersgate Press

3318 Autumn Ridge, Dr., NW, Cleveland, TN 37312

www.holinessandunity.org/aldersgate

To request permissions,
contact the publisher at dhan@ptseminary.edu

ISBN-13: 978-1-955473-01-9 (paperback)

Cover, Images, and Layout by Jeff Del Nero

Printed in the United States of America

For my dear friend,

Kenneth H. Carter, Jr.,

United Methodist Bishop,

in gratitude for his faithful leadership

of the church through the

troubled waters of our days

CONTENTS

Book V (Psalms 107-150)............................150

DAILY PATTERN

Centering Psalm

Wesley Psalms

Wesley Testimony

Silent Reflection

Journaling/Discussion

Prayer & Blessing

INTRODUCTION

On April 1, 2020, in the middle of the COVID-19 pandemic, Bishop Ken Carter posted the following invitation on Facebook:

I'm planning to read five Psalms a day, for the month of April, which will conclude with the 150th Psalm on April 30. We are learning from all epidemiological models that this is going to be a difficult month, and it will call forth spiritual depth, empathy and range of emotion. I would love to find support and accountability from you and I would benefit from all who want to undertake this journey. Most likely I'll read three Psalms in the morning and two in the evening. I may do some journaling and posting here, but reading and praying the Psalms is the core of it for me.

I decided to join in this community of reading, reflection, and prayer, but decided to do it a little differently.

I had always wanted to work my way through Charles Wesley's lyrical paraphrase of the Psalter. While he did not write hymns on all 150 Psalms (he prepared no lyrical paraphrases for Psalms 15, 49, 50, 53, 75, 82, 87, 92, 95, 96, 105, 108, 109, 112, 115, or 148), his Psalm corpus is extensive. He wrote entire hymns on entire Psalms, single-stanza reflections on single verses, and everything in between. He never consolidated this wide-ranging lyrical work into one collection. His 1743 Collection of Psalms and Hymns comes the closest to such a poetic Psalter of his own. Rather, he actually completed his work on many of the Psalms in later years, for example, as when in 1762 he attempted a lyrical paraphrase of the entire Bible. So the selections in this devotional resource are drawn from ten different collections, including a massive Manuscript Psalms compilation. [1] Many of his lyrical paraphrases of the Psalms are magnificent. They bring the ancient Psalms to life in new ways. So I devoted myself to this soul-enriching pilgrimage through Wesley's lyrical material.

As a daily routine, and having attempted previously to read through all 150 Psalms over the course of a month, I found this to be very rewarding, but taxing. While such a reading (and chanting) of these songs remains standard practice in many monastic communities, this large body of prayer contains so much to ponder and absorb. Just reflecting on one Psalm a day meditatively can pull your heart and mind in many directions (and I do not recommend that you begin with Psalm 119, the longest chapter in the Bible). So knowing that most people would find it difficult to read through all Wesley's Psalm hymns in 30 days, I decided to provide a careful selection of stanzas from Wesley's hymns for reflection and prayer. Many people, eager to immerse themselves in the Psalms, can devote time to the reading of a stanza or two of five hymns each day. Determining which stanzas to include was, in itself, a profound religious experience for me. I learned a lot about my own spirituality through that exercise. My hope is that the hymn stanzas I have included here speak to your heart.

I do not need to overwhelm you with background relat-

---

[1] The entire corpus of Charles Wesley's published and manuscript hymns is available online and free of charge at The Center for Studies in the Wesleyan Tradition, Duke Divinity School: *https://divinity.duke.edu/initiatives/cswt*. I offer my heartfelt thanks to Dr. Randy and Aileen Maddox who compiled and annotated this resource. All my modernized adaptations of the Wesley texts used in this volume are based on the lyrical material in this definitive compilation.

ed to Wesley's hymns. They possess a beauty of their own that requires no explanation. But just a few points to set the stage might be helpful. As a devout priest of the Church of England, the Psalms figured prominently in Charles's own devotional life. There is little doubt that he knew most of the Psalms, if not all of them, by heart. They were a regular part of his life of prayer. He followed the pattern of praying the Psalms recommended in the Services of Morning and Evening Prayer of the Book of Common Prayer. He apparently intended many of his lyrical paraphrases of the Psalms for singing—and not just meditative reading—since their meters conform to the tunes of the widely-used 1780 Collection of Hymns. But how did he view the Psalms? What do his hymn settings reveal about his interpretation of the Psalms? S T Kimbrough, Jr. identifies four of Wesley's interpretive approaches to the Psalms that, if kept in mind, can enhance your devotional journey through his hymns. [2] **1|** He understands the Psalms through the lens of the New Testament. Because of this, Christ appears in his Psalm hymns despite the fact that Jesus was born centuries later. **2|** On the other hand, he permits the Psalms to remain the heartfelt songs of the Hebrew people in their original setting. **3|** He contextualizes the Psalms so they fit his contemporary situation. I have followed his lead in this regard as I have modernized his hymns for our use today. **4|** He interprets the Psalms through the lens of a preacher and evangelist. He uses these hymns to introduce the seeker to God and to offer guidance to the Christian disciple. So keep your eyes open for these particular characteristics as you read through and meditate on this lyrical material.

---

[2] S T Kimbrough, Jr., "Directions of Interpretation in Charles Wesley's Psalm Poetry,"Proceedings of The Charles Wesley Society 16 (2012): 29-59.

A couple other important notes concerning these hymns. Charles Wesley was a poet of the 18th century. So the flow of his language, and even some of the terms he uses, are outmoded and archaic to our ears. So I have modernized these selections thoroughly while always attempting to retain the beauty of the originals. I have replaced "thy" and "thine" with "you" and "your;" "may" and "can" displace "mayest" and "canst;" even "heav'nly quires" become more understandably "heavenly choirs." While Wesley was remarkably egalitarian for his day, gendered language about God and humanity permeates his hymns. So I have carefully navigated these kinds of changes as well. Altering the language in these ways does present some major challenges, but here again, I hope I have not done a disservice to the beauty of his original poetry.

Bishop Carter issued this invitation during the time in which many people were called to "shelter in place" during the pandemic. Imposed isolation—its change in normal patterns and pace of life—provides an amazing opportunity for people to connect with God and each other more deeply. I am sure this was Bishop Carter's intention, along with his concern that we "live deeply" through unprecedented times. The title, Sheltering with the Psalms, therefore, relates directly to this experience. But the truth of the matter is that sheltering with the Psalms works in any time, any place, any situation. So I offer this to you as a gift. Immerse yourself in these lyrical paraphrases of the Psalms. Take this journey into the amazing insights of the Psalmist filtered through the brilliant poetry of a godly man. Open your heart to God's presence in a new way.

My instructions to you are very simple. Those who engage in spiritual practices regularly know the importance of space, time, and even posture. Find or create a space in which to reflect and pray. Hopefully it is a quiet place where you can be still and as undisturbed as possible. Meeting with God in this space at the same time each day can really be helpful to the process of settling your spirit. Many people find the early morning the best time for prayer and reflection. Others prefer the evening. But you need to determine what works best for you with regard to your circumstances and daily rhythms. Even posture can be helpful in terms of focus. In my own experience, my general rule in this regard is comfort. Relax. Settle in. This is not a test. Be gracious with yourself and open to the Spirit. Simply prepare to spend some quality time with the God you love—and who loves you deeply—as if you are spending time with a cherished friend.

I do invite you to read this book following a Daily Pattern. It is very simple, consisting of six elements. I have provided a brief centering Psalm to begin your time of sheltering with the Psalms. Simply read the verse and spend a few moments in silence as you begin, inviting the Holy Spirit to open your heart to God's presence. Next, read through the selections from Wesley Psalms. You may want to pause at the conclusion of each, asking yourself what aspects of the hymn touch you or relate to you most directly. The Wesley Testimony that follows consists of excerpts from Charles Wesley's journal or adaptations of his narrative in the form of story. Each testimony aligns with the Psalm selections for the day, either by virtue of the themes or by Wesley's actual allusion to one of the Psalms in the daily entries in his journal account. After having read the Psalms and testimony, embrace just a few moments of Silent Reflection. Let the words and images that linger revolve around naturally in your heart and mind. Be attentive to how this makes you feel. Let God's love flow around you, over you, and through you. I provide several questions and space in the book, then, for personal Journaling or for the purposes of Discussion if you are using this resource in a small group. Use these questions as works best for you. They are meant to prompt reflection; you need not be slavish in following them. You may even prefer simply to journal freely on the basis of your own internal direction. Feel free to mark this book up with your comments and reflections as the Spirit leads. Before you conclude each day's reflection with the Blessing from a Psalm provided, you may want to spend just a few moments with God in Prayer from your heart through the Spirit. Whatever way you decide to bring this time of fellowship with God to a close, do open your heart to receive God's rich blessing on your day and on your life.

Book One: **Psalms 1-41**

"He leads me beside still waters"

Ps 23

Day 1

Centering Psalm

"Blessed are all who take refuge in God" (2:11)

Psalm 1

The Two Ways

2. Obedience is a pure delight,
    Of those who seek to please the Lord:
Their every act through day and night
    To search the soul-converting Word,
The law of liberty to prove,
The perfect law of life and love.

3. Close to the streams of paradise,
    By living water we do grow:
The tree of righteousness shall rise,
    And all its blossoms honor show,
Spread out its boughs, and flourish fair,
And fruit unto perfection bear.

Psalm 2

God's Promise to God's Anointed

2. Earth's haughty kings their Lord oppose,
The rulers call themselves God's foes,
To fight against their God agree,
And slay the incarnate deity.

3. As sworn their Maker to dethrone,
And Jesus, God's anointed Son,
To rise from all subjection freed,
And reign almighty in God's stead.

4. The Lord that calmly sits above
Enthroned in everlasting love,
Shall all their feeble threats deride,
And laugh to scorn their furious pride.

13. Thrice happy all who trust the Lord,
All-good almighty, all-adored;
They only shall God's mercy prove,
Loved with an everlasting love.

WESLEY TESTIMONY

Charles Wesley filled his journal with testimony to God's law of love. On Monday, June 5, 1738, he wrote: "I waked thankful with power to pray and praise... In the afternoon I met Mrs Syms with Mr and Mrs Barton at Islington. He told me God had given him faith, while I was praying last night, but he thought it would do hurt to declare it then. Upon finding his heart burn within him, he desired God would show him some token of his faith and immediately opened on 'Let there be light and there was light' [Gen 1:3]. We rejoiced together in prayer and singing, and left the rest of the company much stirred up to wait for the same unspeakable gift."

Questions for Thought or Discussion

Wesley celebrates "The perfect law of life and love." What does this phrase mean to you and how do you seek to live this out?

The Psalmist describes our lives like "trees planted by streams of water." What is the condition of your tree today; what is the state of your growth?

Where have you seen God's rule of everlasting love recently in these days?

Blessing

"I will tell of the decree of God,
who said to me,
'You are my child;
today I have begotten you'"
(2:7)

Day 2

Centering Psalm

*"O God, our Sovereign,
how majestic is your name
in all the earth" (8:1).*

Psalm 3

Trust in God under Adversity

3. To the Lord I cried; the cry
Brought my helper from the sky;
By my kind protector kept,
Safe I laid me down and slept,
Slept within God's arms, and rose;
Blessed God for the calm repose.

Psalm 4

Confident Plea for Deliverance from Enemies

1. God of my righteousness,
Your humble suppliant hear,
You have relieved me in distress,
And you are always near.
Again your mercy show,
The peaceful answer send,
Assuage my grief, relieve my woe,
And all my troubles end.

Psalm 5
Trust in God for Deliverance from Enemies

1. O Lord, incline your gracious ear,
    My plaintive sorrows weigh,
To you for comfort I draw near,
    To you I humbly pray.
Still will I call with lifted eyes,
    Come, O my God, and King,
Till you regard my ceaseless cries,
    And full deliverance bring.

Psalm 6
Prayer for Recovery from Grave Illness

4. Weary of my unanswered groans;
Yet still with never-ceasing moans
    I languish for relief,
With tears I wash my couch and bed,
My strength is spent, my beauty fled,
    My life worn out with grief.

Psalm 7
Plea for Help against Persecutors

4. Shorn of all my strength I languish;
    See, I faint beneath my load,
Faint through deep distress and anguish,
    Faint—into the arms of God!
God to me in great compassion
    Does a gracious token give,
I shall see God's whole salvation,
    I shall all God's love retrieve.

Psalm 8

Divine Majesty and Human Dignity

1. Sovereign, everlasting Lord,
    How excellent your name!
Held in being by your word,
    You all your works proclaim:
Through this earth your glories shine,
    Through those dazzling worlds above,
All confess the source divine,
    The almighty God of love.

WESLEY TESTIMONY

In November 1739 Charles Wesley preached on a tour through Wales with the great evangelist Howell Harris. At Glamorgan, he expounded the story of the woman of Canaan (Matt 15:22-28), reporting that a spirit of love led him to plead with tears for all those gathered to receive Christ Jesus. A spirit of love ran throughout the entire assembly. He described God's Word as a fire that melted the rocks. God had brought him to that place for this very reason. That evening when he laid down to take his rest, the words of Psalm 4:8 fell upon his heart: "I will both lie down and sleep in peace; for you alone, O God, make me lie down in safety."

Questions for Thought or Discussion

When have you cried out to God for deliverance most recently and how did God respond?

Three words in Psalm 6 describe the reality for many: "I am weary." If you are feeling weary today, what weighs heavily on you?

Have you ever fallen "into the arms of God?" What did that feel like?

Prayer & Blessing:

"You have put gladness in my heart more than when their grain and wine abound.
I will both lie down and sleep in peace;
for you alone, O God, make me lie down in safety" (4:7-8).

Day 3

"Rise up, O God; O God, lift up your hand;
do not forget the oppressed" (10:12).

Psalm 9

God's Power and Justice

1. You I will praise with all my soul,
Your goodness e'er to all extol,
    How marvelous your works of grace:
Your name I will in songs record,
And joy and glory in my Lord,
    Extolled above all thanks and praise.

When you have put my foes to flight,
They all shall feel your utmost might,
    And lose their being with their power,
My foes shall at your presence fall,
My sins shall fade and perish all,
    My sins shall die to live no more.

Psalm 10

Prayer for Deliverance from Enemies

2. Arise, O Lord, arise,
    O God, lift up your hand,
No longer seem to slight our cries,
    But all our foes withstand.
    The poor in their distress

Commit themselves to you,
O helper of the parentless,
    O friend who sees us through.

Psalm 11
Song of Trust in God

1. On the Lord my soul is stayed,
    Wherefore do you bid me fly
To the mountain-top for aid?
    My strong mountain still is nigh,
Jesus' arms are my defense:
Who shall come, and pluck me thence?

Psalm 12
Plea for Help in Evil Times

1. Help, O Lord, the faithful fail,
    No one here continues just,
Shall the gates of hell prevail,
    Shall the church on earth be lost?

8. You, O Lord, shall all fulfil,
    Earth and hell a while may rage,
You are our preserver still,
    Christ is ours from age to age.

Psalm 13

Prayer for Deliverance from Enemies

1. How long will you forget me,
     Lord, will you forever hide your face?
How long will you forget me,
Leave me unchanged, and unrestored,
     An alien from your life of grace!

Psalm 14

Denunciation of Godlessness

1. The fools have in their hearts denied
The God from whom they cannot hide:
Corrupt is the whole human race,
Not one the Maker-God obeys,
Plunged in the depth of Adam's fall, death,
Wrath, and curse o'rewhelm them all.

Wesley was committed to social justice. His vision of the Christian life included faith *and* holiness—conversion to God and active love of neighbor. He illustrated this commitment with the testimony of George White-field. "Monday, October 25, 1756. He preached universally as my brother. He warned them everywhere against apostasy, and strongly insisted on the necessity of holiness *after* justification, illustrating it with this comparison: 'What good would the King's pardon do a poor malefactor dying of a fever? So, notwithstanding you have received forgiveness, unless the disease of your nature be healed by holiness, ye can never be saved.'"

Questions for Thought or Discussion

The Psalms make clear that God's works of grace include both personal salvation and justice in the world. How do you seek to bring balance to these in your life?

Have you ever felt like God forgot about you? If so, how did you deal with that feeling?

Psalm 14 declares that fools say in their hearts "There is no God." What can you do to help such "fools" find God?

Prayer & Blessing

"I trusted in your steadfast love; my heart shall rejoice in your salvation.
I will sing to God, because God has dealt bountifully with me"
(13:5-6).

Day 4

> *"Guard me as the apple of the eye; hide me*
> *in the shadow of your wings" (17:8).*

Psalm 16
Song of Trust and Security in God

7. O God, my heart does now rejoice,
I wait to hear your quickening voice,
    My flesh exults in hope,
You will not leave me in the grave,
Sure confidence in you I have,
    That you will raise me up.

Psalm 17
Prayer for Deliverance from Persecutors

4. Still support me in your ways,
    And my foot shall never fall;
You have heard my calls for grace,
    You will hear me when I call;
Bow your ear, in mercy bow,
Hear me, Lord, and hear me now.

Psalm 18

Royal Thanksgiving for Victory

1. You will I love, O Lord my power:
    My rock and fortress is the Lord,
My God, my Savior, and my tower,
    My horn and strength, my shield and sword;
Secure I trust in God's defense,
I stand in God's omnipotence.

Psalm 19

God's Glory in Creation and the Law

10. The statutes of the Lord are right,
God's laws and equity unite,
Reason divine in all is showed,
Adjusted to the creature's good
They bring us peace, and joy impart,
When written on the obedient heart.

Ten years after his experience of God's unconditional love, Charles's preaching was coming into full flower. In May 1749 he writes glowingly about his experiences of God in the context of proclaiming the Word. Often solemn and joyous celebrations of Holy Communion accompany his deep sense of God's presence. On May 7 he preached at the London Foundery from Psalm 16:12: "You will show me the path of life." He describes how the Word was truly a means of grace to everyone's soul. After preaching, he felt "very great love" as he met with the members of the Society. His experiences of God daily confirmed that he was on the right path.

Questions for Thought or Discussion

The language of God "guarding" and "hiding" is pervasive in the Psalms. What feelings do these images stir up in you?

Wesley sings "Sure confidence in you [God] I have." Has your confidence in God ever been shaken? Reflect or talk about those experiences.

Wesley's paraphrase of Psalm 18 includes some potent images: rock, fortress, tower, horn, strength, shield, sword. Which of these resonates with your experience, and why?

Prayer & Blessing

"In my distress I called upon God; to my God I cried for help. From the temple God heard my voice, and my cry reached God's ears" (18:6).

Day 5

Centering Psalm

"God is my shepherd, I shall not want" (23:1).

Psalm 20
Prayer for Victory

4. Some in chariots put their trust,
    In horses some confide,
We of God will make our boast,
    And in God's Word abide:
God we ever bear in mind,
    All God's faithful mercies claim,
Life, and strength, and victory find
    In Jesus' conquering name.

Psalm 21
Thanksgiving for Victory

6. Eternally blessed, And joyful in you,
Admitted to rest, Your grandeur to view,
They trust in their Savior: Who then shall remove
Their souls from your favor,
    Their hearts from your love?

Psalm 22

Plea for Deliverance from Suffering and Hostility

1. My God, my God, I cry to you,
Am I to be forsaken too,
   Who still lament and groan!
Far from my passionate complaint
Why have you suffered me to faint,
   And seem forever gone!

Psalm 23

The Divine Shepherd

1. Jesus the Good Shepherd is,
   Jesus died the sheep to save:
He is mine, and I am his,
   All I want in him I have,
Life, and health, and rest, and food,
All the plenitude of God.

2. Jesus loves and guards his own,
   Me in verdant pastures feeds,
Makes me quietly lie down,
   By the streams of comfort leads:
Following him, where'er he goes,
Silent joy my heart o'reflows.

3. He in sickness makes me whole,
   Guides into the paths of peace,
He revives my fainting soul,
   Makes me glad and virtuous;
Who for me concedes to die,
Loves me still—I know not why.

6. Love divine shall still embrace,
   Love shall keep me to the end,
Surely all my happy days
   I shall in your temple spend,
Till I to your house remove,
Your eternal house above.

Psalm 24
Entrance into the Temple

1. The earth and all her fulness owns
   Jehovah for her sovereign Lord;
The countless daughters and God's sons
   Rose into being at God's word.

2. God's word did out of nothing call
   The world, and founded all that is,
Launched into space this earthly ball,
   Its fertile land and sparkling seas.

12 Lift up your heads, O heavenly gates,
   O everlasting doors give way. . . .

13 Who is this King of Glory, who?
   The Lord of glorious power possessed,
The King of saints and angels too,
   God over all, forever blessed.

WESLEY TESTIMONY

Visiting the sick was an important ministry in early Methodism. Charles Wesley was called to the bed of a young woman who was deathly ill. She eagerly told him about a vision she had experienced several days before. She saw herself, as it were, dropping further and further away from God. Suddenly, a ray of light darted into her soul and filled her with all peace and joy in believing. All fear of hell, death, and sin fled away in that same moment. Wesley recited the Twenty-third Psalm with her and reminded her of God's promise to those who walk through the valley of the shadow of death. They will fear no evil.

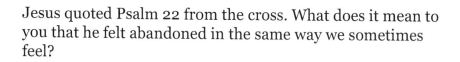

Questions for Thought or Discussion

Jesus quoted Psalm 22 from the cross. What does it mean to you that he felt abandoned in the same way we sometimes feel?

Without question, Psalm 23 is the most famous of all these songs of faith. What has this Psalm meant to you over the years?

Many of the Psalms, like 24, reflect our life of worship. How do you worship in times of isolation or separation? How can you connect with God and the community of faith?

Prayer & Blessing

"Surely goodness and mercy shall follow me all the days of my life, and I shall dwell in the house of God my whole life long" (23:6).

Day 6

Centering Prayer

> *"Lead me in your truth, and teach me,*
> *for you are the God of my salvation;*
> *for you I wait all day long" (25:5).*

Psalm 25

Prayer for Guidance and Deliverance

2. Your ways to me, O Jesus, show,
And teach me in your paths to go,
    Direct my willing heart,
O God of my salvation, lead
A soul that in your steps would tread,
    Nor evermore depart.

Psalm 26

Plea for Justice and Declaration of Righteousness

7. Here on your promise, Lord,
    My anchored faith stands sure,
My soul is tethered to your Word;
    Till you have made me pure,
    Then will I bless your name,
    Till joined to you above,
The length, and breadth, and height proclaim,
    And depth of sovereign love.

Psalm 27

Triumphant Song of Confidence

1. The Lord my great salvation is,
My life, and health, my joy, and peace,
　　My light, my comfort, and my power,
Whom shall I now submit to fear?
Though hell, the world, and sin are near,
　　They never shall my soul devour.

To swallow up my soul they came,
But armed with faith in Jesus' name
　　I more than conquered them in fight;
They stumbled on my Rock and fell;
And should their host again assail,
　　I scorn to fear their baffled might.

2. I trust in Jesus Christ, my Lord,
He shall fulfil his gracious word,
　　And grant the blessing I require,
That I throughout my happy days
May in his house record his praise
　　This, this is all my heart's desire.

Still in God's hallowed courts to dwell,
To see the great Invisible,
　　And ever on God's beauties gaze,
The channels of God's grace attend,
Till grace mature in glory end,
　　And I in heaven behold God's face.

Psalm 28

Prayer for Help and Thanksgiving for It

5. Lord Christ, my heart with joy is filled,
And dances to your blessed name,
    You are my more than sevenfold shield;
In songs my Helper I proclaim,
The strength of all that trust in him,
    All-good Almighty to redeem.

Psalm 29

The Voice of God in the Great Storm

4. Enthroned in power our Savior sits,
And earth to the great King submits,
    All heaven its sovereign Lord adores;
And at God's glorious throne we bow,
Desirous of full healing now—
    God all our strength divine restores.

Jesus to all who dare believe,
The fulness of his power shall give,
    The gospel-hope, the glorious prize,
The perfect love, the perfect peace,
The everlasting righteousness,
    The heaven-insuring paradise.

WESLEY TESTIMONY

"Faith" permeated the preaching of Charles Wesley. Faith anchors the soul, liberates the heart, and restores love. These themes echo in his journal entries throughout August 1743. "The great power of God was, meantime, among us, overturning all before it, and melting our hearts into contrite, joyful love... At four took my leave of the Society, with that apostolic prayer: 'And the very God of peace sanctify you wholly,' etc. [1 Thes 5:23]. Great peace was upon them all. Their prayers and tears of love I shall never forget... At eight preached faith in Christ. Their tears and hearty expressions of love convince me there is a work begun in their hearts."

Questions for Thought or Discussion

With regard to Psalm 27, Wesley sings, "My anchored faith stands sure, / My soul is tethered to your Word." What is the connection between the Word and your faith?

Wesley uses the terms life, health, joy, peace, light, comfort, and power to describe salvation. Which of these resonates the most with you right now, and why?

What is making your heart dance today in the midst of the storm?

Prayer & Blessing

"God is my light and my salvation; whom shall I fear? God is the stronghold of my life; of whom shall I be afraid (27:1)?

Day 7

Be strong, and let your heart take courage,
all you who wait for God" (31:24).

Psalm 30
Thanksgiving for Recovery from Grave Illness

4. If we wait for answered prayers,
    Feeling left all night to mourn,
Wondering if God really cares,
    Wondering if God shall return.
Sure as the return of day
    Chases all the shades of night,
Sorrow does to joy give way,
    Darkness to the gospel-light.

8. You have filled my life with joy,
    That I might my Lord proclaim,
All my days in thanks employ,
    Sing, and bless your glorious name:
Surely this my joy shall be
    Till I join the hosts above,
Plunged into the Deity,
    Lost in all the depths of love.

Psalm 31

Prayer and Praise for Deliverance from Enemies

1. In you, O Lord, we trust,
     And in your saving name,
   Faithful, and to your promise just,
     O rid us of our shame:
     O never, never leave
     Us sinners to our sin,
   Who would your gracious word receive,
     And long to be made clean.

2. In condescending love
     Incline your ear to me,
   Send down the answer from above,
     And haste to set me free:
     O be my rock, my tower,
     To which I still may fly,
   Redeem me, Savior, by your power,
     Redeem me, or I die.

Psalm 32

The Joy of Forgiveness

9 O faithful soul, joy in your Lord,
     Whose arms are still your sure defense,
   Your great redeemer is our God:
     Believe; and who shall pluck you thence?
   O child of upright heart be glad,
     For Jesus is your God and friend,
   God keeps whoe'er on Christ is stayed,
     And Christ shall keep them to the end.

Psalm 33

The Greatness and Goodness of God

1. Righteous souls, rejoice in God,
    Right it is for you to praise
God, who has the gift bestowed,
    Made you vessels of God's grace:
Praise the Lord, O Saints, and sing,
    All your sacred skill exert,
All the powers of music bring:
    Praise God with a thankful heart.

2. Sing the new, the good-news song,
    Make a loud and cheerful noise,
Praise does all to God belong,
    In God's faithful Word rejoice.
All God's works are good and right;
    Only such can God approve,
Righteousness is God's delight,
    Earth is full of God's great love.

WESLEY TESTIMONY

May 21, 1738 was a major turning point in Charles Wesley's life. His conversion experience on that Pentecost Sunday preceded the more famous "heart-warming experience" of his brother, John, which occurred three days later. Hearing the words of Psalm 32:1—"Happy are those whose transgression is forgiven"—figured prominently in the transforming work of the Holy Spirit on that day. "I now found myself at peace with God, and rejoiced in hope of loving Christ," he testified. "I saw that by faith I stood; by the continual support of faith, which kept me from falling."

Questions for Thought or Discussion

Reflect on an experience in which you "wept through the night" but were surprised by "joy in the morning."

The Psalms deal openly with the issue of sin in our lives and the deliverance God offers. What experiences of deliverance have you had?

The last two Psalms for this day celebrate the joy that comes with the experience of forgiveness. How has offering forgiveness to others or receiving this gift filled you with joy?

Prayer & Blessing

"You have turned my mourning into dancing;
you have taken off my sackcloth and clothed me with joy,
so that my soul may praise you and not be silent. O God my God, I will give thanks to you forever" (30:11-12).

Day 8

Centering Psalm

*"O taste and see that God is good;
happy are those who take refuge in God" (34:8)*

Psalm 34
Praise for Deliverance from Trouble

2. All humble followers of the Lord,
   With me exalt God's praise,
Join humankind with sweet accord
   To glorify God's grace.
I sought God, and God kindly heard
   The sinner in distress,
And ransomed me from all I feared,
   And bade me go in peace.

4. All those who humbly fear the Lord
   Angelic hosts attend,
And ministerial spirits guard
   And keep them to the end.
O taste, dear Christ-less soul, and see
   The Lord how good and kind!
God reaches out with good to me,
   To all of humankind!

Psalm 35

Prayer for Deliverance from Enemies

4. With your shield my weakness cover,
   Guard my head by your aid
   'Till the storm is over.

6. All the power of pride and passion
   O control, tell my soul
   I am your salvation.

7. Then my soul shall bow before you,
   Spread your praise, sing your grace,
   And with thanks adore you.

8. My whole soul, my strength, shall bless you,
   All I am shall proclaim,
   And with joy confess you.

Psalm 36

Human Wickedness and Divine Goodness

3. O you, my Lord, are full of grace,
Above the clouds your mercies rise,
Steadfast your truth and faithfulness,
Your word of promise never dies,
Nor earth can shake, nor hell remove
The base of your eternal love.

4. Unsearchable your judgments are,
A boundless bottomless abyss:
But, lo! Your providential care

O'er all your works extended is;
In you the creatures live and move,
And are: All glory to your love!

Psalm 37
Exhortation to Patience and Trust

12. In paths of righteousness
    God leads all servants right,
Those servants' steady walk
    God sees with favor and delight:
    Though into trouble cast
    They shall not fall away,
The Lord supports and holds them fast,
    And shall forever stay.

20. The Lord rewards God's own,
    With heavenly happiness;
And saves them till their course is run,
    Supports them in distress:
    All those who struggle on,
    A present Savior have,
God never has God's grace withdrawn,
    God shall forever save.

WESLEY TESTIMONY

Wesley had a preaching appointment among the miners in Kingswood. He and his friends were in a carriage, just ready to step out, when the horse bolted and overturned everything. Wesley leapt over both the horse and the carriage, but one of the women in their company was thrown out on her head and the carriage turned topsy turvy over her. She lay beneath the wheels, untouched by either, and the horse lay quiet on his back. All of them got up, completely unharmed. Psalm 36:6 sprang to Charles's mind: "You save humans and animals alike, O Lord." The thought of the excellence of God's mercy overwhelmed him!

Questions for Thought or Discussion

Deliverance figures prominently in the first two Psalms for today. Describe a situation in which God delivered you from danger, difficulty, or death—jeopardy of any kind.

Psalm 36 discusses God's "providential care." How have you felt cared for by God and others in the living of these days?

Patience is a virtue. How have these days helped or hindered your cultivation of patience?

Prayer & Blessing

"Your steadfast love, O God, extends to the heavens, your faithfulness to the clouds. Your righteousness is like the mighty mountains, your judgments are like the great deep; you save humans and animals alike, O God" (36:5-6).

Day 9

"Do not forsake me, O God; O my God,
do not be far from me; make haste to help me,
O God, my salvation" (38:21-22).

Psalm 38

A Patient Sufferer's Plea for Healing

6. Lord, all my wants to you are known,
You always hear my every groan,
     You see my desperate case;
My panting heart has lost its might,
My weeping eyes have lost their light,
     Nor view your blissful face.

12. Ah! Leave me not, my God and Lord,
Defer not to fulfil your word,
     Nor from my soul remove,
Make haste your goodness to reveal,
And let me my salvation feel
     In all-forgiving love.

Psalm 39

Prayer for Wisdom and Forgiveness

5. You have numbered out my days,
     Life is like a grain of sand,
Shorter than a moment's space,
     Nothing can my life expand;
Generations come and go,
All is vanity below.

7. Grieved by efforts here to grope,
     What do I expect below?
Lord, in you I place my hope,
     You alone I want to know,
Wait to taste how good you are,
Long to see the Morning Star.

11. Hear O Lord, my mournful prayer,
      O regard my earnest cry,
Do not still your help defer,
      Send me comfort from on high,
Hear my clamorous griefs and fears,
Answer all my silent tears.

Psalm 40

Thanksgiving for Deliverance and Prayer for Help

5. No phantom form do you require,
     No legal sacrifice approve,
You seek the contrite heart's desire,
     The offering of obedient love,
And lo! I come to do your will,
And all your law in love fulfill.

8. The great salvation you have wrought
     I have with joy to all declared:
Ah dearest Lord, forsake me not,
     But let your tender mercies guard,
Your faithful love my soul defend,
And save and keep me to the end.

Psalm 41

Assurance of God's Help and a Plea for Healing

7. O raise me up, my gracious God,
   That I my wish may see,
The evil by my good subdued,
   All souls brought home and free.
I know full well your favor Lord,
   Because, your grace again
Has raised me up, and through your word
   My victory maintain.

8. You keep me now from hour to hour,
   And set before your face,
To sing the greatness of your power,
   And triumph in your praise.
Glory to Israel's God and Lord
   God's name exalted be
By angels and by saints adored
   To all eternity.

WESLEY TESTIMONY

On the day of Charles Wesley's conversion, the Holy Spirit led him to two Psalms in addition to Psalm 32, as alluded to above. God's Word was softening his heart and elevating his sense of hope. In his journal Charles describes the way in which he simply opened his Bible when he arose from his bed. The first words that met his eyes were: "And now, O Lord, what do I wait for? My hope is in you" (Psalm 39:7). He took a deep breath, and his eyes fell on the words of Psalm 40:3: "He put a new song in my mouth, a song of praise to our God. Many will see and fear, and put their trust in the Lord." Faith as trust welled up in his heart.

Questions for Thought or Discussion

Wesley's hymn on Psalm 38 includes the pleas "make haste to help" and "make haste to reveal your goodness." The singer's heart is urgent. What is your urgency today?

Psalm 39 continues this sense of urgency, reminding us how short life really is. Pushed to think about the "most important things," what is your list of absolute essentials in life?

More than anything else, God desires you heart. What action can you take today to make sure your heart is aligned with the heart of God?

Prayer & Blessing

*"You have multiplied, O
God my God,
your wondrous deeds and
your thoughts toward us;none
can compare with you. Were
I to proclaim and tell of them,
they would be more than can
be counted" (40:5).*

Book Two: **Psalms 42-72**

"Create
in me
a clean
heart"

Ps 51

Day 10

Centering Psalm

"As a deer longs for flowing streams,
so my soul longs for you, O God" (42:1).

Psalm 42

Longing for God and God's Help in Distress

1. As the hart from flying faint
For the cooling stream does pant,
So my soul by sin pursued
Pants for you the living God.

7. I shall yet record God's praise,
My voice in praise of grace I'll raise,
When mercy vanquishes my fears,
When the face of God appears.

10. Deep to deep with horror calls,
While the roaring torrent falls,
My abyss of misery
calls on grace to set me free.

15. I shall yet record God's praise,
See again the Savior's face,
Ascertained by love divine,
Mine God is, forever mine!

Psalm 43
Prayer to God in Time of Trouble

3. O my merciful redeemer,
    Show the brightness of your face,
Let your love be my protector,
    Lead me by the light of grace.
Send the unction of your Spirit,
    Guide into your perfect will,
That I may your heaven inherit,
    Meet you on your holy hill.

5. Wherefore then, my restless spirit,
    Are you troubled and cast down?
Hope in God, through Jesus' merit,
    God through Jesus is your own;
I shall yet retrieve God's favor,
    I shall sing God's praise aloud,
Jesus is my loving Savior,
    Jesus is my pardoning God!

Psalm 44
National Lament and Prayer for Help

12. Our soul is to the dust bowed down,
    Our belly to the earth does cleave,
Hear your afflicted people groan,
    And for your mercy sake relieve:
Arise, your great salvation show,
    Our foes confound, our shame remove,
That all the world with us may know
    Your utmost power of saving love.

Psalm 45

Ode for a Royal Wedding

8. O God of love, your power we own,
    Your dying love does all control;
Justice and grace support your throne,
    Set up in every faithful soul,
Steadfast it stands in them, and sure,
When pure as you their God are pure.

18 Adorned with purity and love,
    With every dazzling virtue bright,
With faith its character to prove,
    A precious church in God's own sight,
The royal maid with joy shall come,
Triumphant to her heavenly home.

21 O Jesus, King of kings, and Lord
    Of lords, I glory to proclaim,
From age to age your praise record,
    That all the world may learn your name:
And all shall soon your grace adore,
When time and sin shall be no more.

WESLEY TESTIMONY

On July 17, 1741 Wesley was particularly moved by his sense of the presence of the Holy Spirit among the poor people who accepted his invitation to hear him preach at Kingswood. He talks about how these poorest of the poor ate their food with gladness, feeding figuratively on the Word and, literally, as they shared a meal together. He pondered Psalm 42 and the ways in which sounds of praise and thanksgiving filled the homes of these humble people. They were singing in every room. Particularly in the kitchen, those at work lifted their voices in praise. He says that he felt as if he were in the house of Abraham.

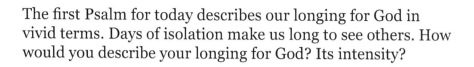
Questions for Thought or Discussion

The first Psalm for today describes our longing for God in vivid terms. Days of isolation make us long to see others. How would you describe your longing for God? Its intensity?

"Why are you cast down, O my Soul" (Psalm 43:5). Is that your question today? Where can you find hope today, if that is the case; how can you lift the spirits of others?

Psalm 45 draws its images from the grandeur of a royal wedding with the dominant themes of purity and love. How do images of covenantal love shape your life?

Prayer & Blessing

"Deep calls to deep at the thunder of your cataracts; all your waves and your billows have gone over me. By day God commands God's steadfast love, and at night God's song is with me, a prayer to the God of my life" (42:7-8).

Day 11

Centering Psalm

"Create in me a clean heart, O God,
and put a new and right spirit within me" (51:10).

Psalm 46
God's Defense of God's City and People

1. God, the omnipresent God,
     Omnipotent, God stands
Ready now relief to afford,
     God's mercy never ends:
Readiest when we need God most,
     When to God distressed we cry,
All who on God's mercy trust
     Shall find deliverance nigh.

4. From the throne of God there springs
     A pure and crystal stream,
Life, and peace, and joy it brings
     To God's Jerusalem:
Rivers of refreshing grace
     Through the sacred city flow,
Watering all the hallowed place
     Where God resides below.

Psalm 47

God's Rule over the Nations

1. Clap your hands, you people all,
Praise the God on whom you call,
Lift your voice, and shout God's praise,
Triumph in God's sovereign grace.

13. Wonderful in saving power
God let all our hearts adore,
Earth and heaven repeat the cry,
"Glory be to God most high!"

Psalm 48

The Glory and Strength of Zion

1. Great is our redeeming Lord
    In power, and truth, and grace,
God by highest heaven adored
    God's church on earth should praise:
In the city of our God,
    In God's holy mount below
Publish, spread God's praise abroad,
    And all God's greatness show.

Psalm 51

Prayer for Cleansing and Parson

11. My secret self to you convert,
Create in me a contrite heart,
    My fallen soul restore,
Let me the life divine attain,
The image of my God regain,
    And never lose it more.

14. Then shall I teach the world your ways,
Your mercy mild and pardoning grace
    For every sinner free,
'Till sinners to your grace submit,
And fall at their redeemer's feet,
    And weep, and love like me.

16. So shall I sing the Savior's name,
Your gift of righteousness proclaim,
    Your all-redeeming grace:
Open my lips, almighty Lord,
That I your mercy may record,
    And glory in your praise.

18. A wounded soul, by sin distressed,
A broken heart that pants for rest,
    This is the sacrifice
Well-pleasing in the sight of God;
A child convicted by your Word,
    You never will despise.

The town of Dartford in Kent developed something of a reputation as a center of military activity. The relationship between the soldiers and the community was not always good! Wesley preached outside the army camp there for several days in November 1745, a year that witnessed serious political upheaval and rebellion. Many of the poor soldiers listened diligently to his words. As the regiment passed his door one day, Wesley took the opportunity of giving each soldier a book. When he preached on God's defense of God's people [Psalm 46], an officer who was present burst into tears, demonstrating the emotion of his heart.

Questions for Thought or Discussion

We all long for "rivers of refreshing grace." How is God's grace refreshing you through these days of sheltering in the Psalms?

The Psalms repeatedly celebrate God's steadfast love. What does that term, "steadfast love," mean to you? How does it differ from other forms of love?

Each of us is a secret self (internal, hidden), a present self (external, projected), and a true self. What cleansing is required for you to grow into your true self as God's child?

Prayer & Blessing

"We ponder your steadfast love, O God, in the midst of your temple. Your name, O God, like your praise, reaches to the ends of the earth. Your right hand is filled with victory" (48:9-10).

Day 12

Centering Prayer

*"Cast your burden on God, who will sustain you,
and will never permit the righteous to be moved" (55:22).*

Psalm 52

Judgment on the Deceitful

12. Savior, I thankfully adore,
And bless and praise you ever more:
You only Lord, the work have done,
Have ransomed me by grace alone.

13. Your mercy still will I proclaim,
And trust, and triumph in your name;
For O! tis all the saints' delight
Till perfect faith is lost in sight.

Psalm 54

Prayer for Vindication

1. Save me, Lord, by your great name,
  Avenge me by your might;
  Hated for your sake I am,
  O vindicate my right;
  Let my prayers your help engage,
Give ear to my continued cry,
  Save me from the oppressor's rage,
  O save me, or I die.

Psalm 55

Complaint about a Friend's Treachery

3. My heart is pained within my breast,
I sink by fear of death oppressed,
    And tremble at my doom,
O'rewhelmed with dread and sore affright,
And horror deep as Egypt's night,
    Or hell's tremendous gloom.

4. O that I from the world could fly,
And 'scape this lowering tempest nigh!
    O that the heavenly Dove
Would lend her wings my flight to aid,
And to some cool, refreshing shade
    My fluttering soul remove!

14. God still the united prayer shall hear,
Again in my behalf appear,
    For God is still the same:
My foes God shall in wrath cast down,
Who will not turn, or fear God's frown,
    Or tremble at God's name.

Psalm 56

Trust in God under Persecution

8. In God I trust, the good, the true:
I will not fear what flesh can do,
 For Jesus takes my part:
I bless you, Savior, for your grace,
Offer my sacrifice of praise,
 And pay you all my heart.

9. For you have saved my soul from death,
From sin, the world, and hell beneath;
 You have my sins forgiven,
That I the glorious light may see,
Walk before God, and perfect be,
 And live the life of heaven.

WESLEY TESTIMONY

Wesley's experience as a missionary in Georgia discouraged him deeply. He found it extremely difficult to adapt to the new climate and life in the fledgling colony. Having been known at Oxford for his friendliness, he recoiled from the constant turmoil of his new relationships. On April 10, 1736 he found encouragement from Psalm 52 that pronounced judgment against the deceitful. Later that day his brother arrived unexpectedly, just at the point he felt he could not go on. John took him aside for a walk and told him that the Spirit blessed him with a word just as he arrived:

"If God is for us, who is against us" (Romans 8:31).

Questions for Thought or Discussion

Words like deceit, treachery, dishonesty, corruption, and ruthlessness pervade this cluster of Psalms. When you encounter these forms of evil in your life, what do you do?

The singer of Wesley's Psalm 54 cries out to God for vindication. Have you ever felt like you were "hated for sake of Christ?" How did you experience the "kingdom of God" in those moments?

When you are "overwhelmed by dread," to whom do you turn? How do you find your way through to the light?

Prayer & Blessing

"You have delivered my soul from death, and my feet from falling, so that I may walk before God in the light of life" *(56:13)*.

Day 13

Centering Psalm

"Be merciful to me, O God, be merciful to me,
for in you my soul takes refuge;
in the shadow of your wings I will take refuge,
until the destroying storms pass by" (57:1).

Psalm 57

Praise and Assurance under Persecution

4. Among the vicious brutes I dwell,
    Fierce as the wildest beasts of prey,
Enflamed with rage like fiends of hell,
    My soul they seek to tear and slay:
As spears their teeth, as darts their words,
Their double tongues are two-edged swords.

7. My heart is fixed, O God, my heart
    Is fixed to triumph in your grace
(Awake my lute, and bear your part,)
    My glory is to sing your praise,
Till of your nature I partake,
And bright in all your image wake.

Psalm 58

Prayer for Vengeance

2. Far from the truth and living way,
Conceived in sin, nursed up in lies,
    The wicked haste to go astray,
And still to bolder mischiefs rise;

Their tongues like serpents stings they dart,
    And vent the poison of their heart.

4. But you, O God, confound their power;
And save the hunted soul from death,
    Baffle when ready to devour,
And break the pouncing lion's teeth,
And just when they their arrows shoot,
    God, then destroy them branch and root.

Psalm 59

Prayer for Deliverance from Enemies

5. Lurking in their dens all day,
    Summoned by the evening hour,
See them ranging for their prey,
    Seeking whom they may devour,
Yelling with infernal yell,
Howling like the dogs of hell.

6. Foul their mouth, and filled with lies,
    Swords are in their lips unclean;
Who regards their perjuries?
    Surely you, O Lord, have seen:
You on them your hand shall turn,
Laugh their idle rage to scorn.

12. Now I will your power confess,
    Early I your love will sing,
God, my refuge in distress,
    Did to me deliverance bring,
You I praise with those above,
God of power and God of love.

Psalm 60

Prayer for National Victory after Defeat

4. E'en now your tender mercy spread
A banner o're your people's head
That all who humbly you revere
May triumph in redemption near.

5. The glorious gospel-truth receive,
And ransomed by your mercy live:
Lord, to your standard—cross I flee,
Stretch out your arm—and ransom me.

6. God in pure holiness has sworn
That all who to their Savior turn
Will all victorious grace then prove,
And more than conquer in his love.

WESLEY TESTIMONY

On April 11, 1736 Wesley continued to strug-
gle with his ordeals in Georgia. His practice
was to pray Morning and Evening Prayer
each day from his Anglican Book of Common
Prayer. This pattern of prayer included a sys-
tematic recitation of the Psalms. This Sunday
morning he recorded in his journal: "What
words could more support our confidence
than the following, out of the Psalms for the
day?" He then transcribed several verses
from Psalm 57 into his journal: "Be merciful
to me, O God, be merciful to me, for in you
my soul takes refuge; in the shadow of your
wings I will take refuge, until the destroying
storms pass by" (verse 1).

Questions for Thought or Discussion

The themes of deliverance and victory over evil resurface in the opening Psalms today. How do Wesley's paraphrases of these Psalms make you feel?

Life can be very brutal. The imagery of "lion's teeth" and "serpent's sting" drive home the realities of evil and injustice. When has abuse felt like this to you?

Have you ever felt like someone else's prey? If so, how were you delivered?

Prayer & Blessing

"God will send from heaven and save me, putting to shame those who trample on me. God will send forth God's steadfast love and faithfulness" (57:3).

Day 14

"O God, you are my God, I seek you, my soul thirsts for you;
my flesh faints for you, as in a dry and weary land where
there is no water" (63:1).

Psalm 61

Assurance of God's Protection

2. You have oft my shelter been,
      My strong defensive tower,
   Saved me from the world and sin,
      And all the accuser's power,
   Still I in your house abide,
And never, never hence remove,
   Still determined to confide
      In your redeeming love.

5. Joyful in this blessed hope
      O glorify your name,
   'Till your mercy take me up
      Your mercy I proclaim,
   Throughout every happy day
On this delightful task attend,
   All I owe in love repay,
      And love you to the end.

Psalm 62

Song of Trust in God Alone

4.But still in patient hope
  My soul on God attend,
And calmly confident look up
  'Till God salvation send;
  [I shall God's goodness see,
  While on God's name I call;]
God now defends and strengthens me,
  And I shall never fall.

6.Trust in the Lord alone
  Who helps us from above
O people all surround God's throne,
  And hang upon God's love:
  Pour out your hearts in prayer,
  And still on God depend,
And God that does your burden bear
  Shall keep you to the end.

Psalm 63

Comfort and Assurance in God's Presence

1. O God, you are in Jesus mine:
For you I sigh, for you I pine
  And pant your power to prove
My longing soul implores your grace,
In a dry barren wilderness
  Un-watered by your love.

3. Your love does all delights exceed,
Your precious love is life indeed;

My lips shall sing your praise:
My hands I lift in Jahweh's name,
My life and strength, and all I am
    Shall glorify your grace.

5. On you I muse with vast delight
Through all the happy sleepless night
    I lean as on your breast
Beneath the shadow of your wing
Jesus my peace, my joy,
    I sing my everlasting rest.

Psalm 64
Prayer for Protection from Enemies

1. Lord, your humble suppliant hear,
Save me, save me from my fear,
From the malice of my foe
Keep me all my days below.

2. O preserve my life above,
Far beyond their reach remove,
From their force and treachery
Set my soul and spirit free.

14. Every child whose heart is right
Shall in Jesus' praise delight,
Glad in him their faith confess
Shout the Lord their righteousness!

The persecution of the Methodists in Wednesbury was fierce. It was here that John Wesley stood down the mob as the ruffians cried out, "Hang him up upon the next tree! Away with him! Kill him." On the morning of October 26, 1743, John and Charles arose before day to sing hymns to Christ as God. As soon as it was light, they walked into town and preached about tribulation. Charles records that it was a most glorious time. Referring to Psalm 63, he claims that their souls were satisfied as with marrow and fatness. He longed for the Lord's coming to confess both he and his brother before God and God's holy angels.

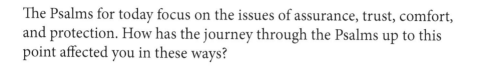

Questions for Thought or Discussion

The Psalms for today focus on the issues of assurance, trust, comfort, and protection. How has the journey through the Psalms up to this point affected you in these ways?

"Lead me to the rock that is higher than I" (Psalm 61:2). How has this journey led you "higher" in your spiritual journey to and with God?

You are nearly at the halfway point of sheltering with the Psalms. Is there a particular hymn of Charles Wesley that stands out? Which Psalm(s) has meant the most to you?

Prayer & Blessing

*"My soul is satisfied as with a
rich feast,
and my mouth praises you
with joyful lips when I think of
you on my bed,
and meditate on you in the
watches of the night; for you
have been my help,
and in the shadow of your
wings I sing for joy"* (63:5-7).

Day 15

Sing to God, sing praises to God's name; lift up a song to God who rides upon the clouds, whose name is the Most High, be exultant before God" (68:4)

Psalm 65
Thanksgiving for Earth's Bounty

9. Full of providential love
   Your children, you sustain,
Send your blessings from above
   In earth-enriching rain,
From your river in the skies
   Streams through airy channels flow,
Bid the springing grain arise,
   And cheer the world below.

11. Springs the watered wilderness
   Into a fruitful field,
Earth her hundred-fold increase
   Does at your bidding yield;
In her freshest mantle clad,
   Springs to life the countryside
All the little hills are glad
   And shout on every side.

Psalm 66

Praise of God's Goodness to Israel

1. O all you lands rejoice in God,
    The God of truth and grace,
God's name we publish now abroad,
    And magnify God's praise. . . .

4. Sing to the Lord, all people sing,
    With us our God proclaim
Let all the wide creation ring
    With praises to God's name.
God keeps our souls, and from God's ways
    God will not let us move,
But feeds us with the life of grace,
    And builds us up in love.

Psalm 67

The Nations Called to Praise God

1. God on us great grace bestow
    Your freely-pardoning grace,
Bless us from our sins, and show
    The brightness of your face.
Let your way on earth be shown,
    You, let every sinner find,
Make your great salvation known
    To all of humankind.

2. Let the people praise you, Lord,
    The God of truth and grace,
You the everlasting Word,
    Let all the people praise.

O give thanks, rejoice, and sing
 Every creature under heaven!
Let them triumph in their King,
 And shout their sins forgiven.

Psalm 68

Praise and Thanksgiving

14. All kingdoms of the earth arise,
Sing unto God, who bows the skies,
 Salute the almighty King of kings,
God from the heaven of heavens comes down,
Forsakes the everlasting throne,
 And grace and peace to sinners brings.

Hear God, all nations, and rejoice,
God's voice God sends, God's mighty voice,
 And bids you enter in and live:
Sinners, receive the gospel-Word,
Your loving, all-redeeming Lord
 With joy let humankind receive.

WESLEY TESTIMONY

Charles Wesley prayed fervently for the conversion of souls. On June 10, 1738, he joined with John Bray in this kind of prayer for Henry Piers. He prayed after God again and again. He reminded Piers about the promises that accompany the prayer of faith. He prayed Psalm 65 and felt every word of it for his friend: "Happy are those whom you choose and bring near to live in your courts. . . . By awesome deeds you answer us with deliverance, O God of our salvation" (verses 4-5). The Spirit broke through and assisted him in prayer. Immediately, the Spirit witnessed with their spirits that their friend's heart was as theirs and all were filled with joy.

Questions for Thought or Discussion

The tone in this cluster of Psalms shifts to thanksgiving and praise. What do you have to be thankful for the most today in praise of God?

These Psalms remind me of the hymn of George Herbert, "Let all the world in every corner sing." What "corners of the world" elicit delight in you?

Note the uplifting verbs in these hymns: God sustains, blesses, feeds, builds. All creation arises, sings, and rings. God's children praise, rejoice, shout, and triumph. How do all these verbs lift your spirits?

*"May God be gracious to us
and bless us and make the
Lord's face to shine upon us,
that your way may be known
upon earth, your saving power among all nations" (67:1-2).*

Day 16

Centering Psalm

"Be pleased, O God, to deliver me.
O Lord, make haste to help me (70:1)!

Psalm 69

Prayer for Deliverance from Persecution

11. Lord, for your mercy sake draw near,
In all your tender love appear,
    Make haste to my relief,
No longer hide from me your face,
But hear, and save me by your grace
    From all my sin and grief.

16. The humble shall behold God's grace,
Your heart shall live who seek God's face,
    Rejoice in steadfast hope,
God never has the poor abhorred,
The mournful prisoners of the Lord
    God hears, and lifts them up.

Psalm 70

Prayer for Deliverance from Enemies

1. Jesus, mighty to deliver,
    Help afford, hasten Lord
        Or I die forever.

2. Those who have my soul surrounded
    Let them flee, chastened be,
        Baffled, and confounded.

3. But let all who seek your favor
    Hear your voice, and rejoice
      In their present Savior.

5. Let them all your acts review,
    Full of praise for your grace
      Let their hearts adore you.

6. O might I with these confess you!
    Needy I fain would try
      With your saints to bless you.

7. Hasten, Lord, my soul deliver;
    Work your cures, Seal me yours,
      Seal me yours forever.

Psalm 71

Prayer for Lifelong Protection and Help

4. The life your tender love bestowed
    Your tender love has still sustained,
You from the womb have been my God,
    The breath which by your grace I gained,
I render back in songs of praise,
I live to glorify your grace.

13. Wherefore I will your goodness sing,
    Your faithfulness with joy record,
My harp, and every tuneful string
    Shall sound the mercies of my Lord,
The Holy One of Israel praise,
The pardoning God of truth and grace.

Psalm 72

Prayer for Guidance and Support for the Ruler

O God in Christ, accept our prayer;
On your disciple here confer
   The wisdom from above,
Your righteousness impute, impart,
And put within this tender heart
   Your law of heavenly love.

WESLEY TESTIMONY

"Deliverance" appears as a repeated theme in Wesley's journal. His main concern was the mob. "Monday, July 18, 1743. When we came to the place of battle, the enemy was ready, set in array against us ... they beating their drum and shouting. I stood still and silent for some time, finding they would not receive my testimony. Then offered to speak to some of the most violent, but they stopped their ears, and ran upon me crying I should not preach there, and catching at me to pull me down.

My soul was calm and fearless. I walked leisurely through the thickest of them, who followed like ramping and roaring lions—but their mouth was shut."

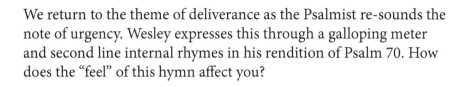

Questions for Thought or Discussion

We return to the theme of deliverance as the Psalmist re-sounds the note of urgency. Wesley expresses this through a galloping meter and second line internal rhymes in his rendition of Psalm 70. How does the "feel" of this hymn affect you?

Wesley uses the language of "tender love" in the excerpts from Psalm 71. In your personal journey, who has exhibited this kind of love toward you?

In Psalm 72 the adjective "tender" appears again, but here in reference to the heart. How has reading through and meditating upon the Psalms "softened" your heart?

Prayer & Blessing

"Let the oppressed see it and be glad; you who seek God, let your hearts revive.
For God hears those who are needy, and does not despise God's own that are in bonds" (69:32-33).

30 DAYS OF PRAYER WITH CHARLES WESLEY   111

Book Three: **Psalms 73-89**

"The glorious deeds of the Lord"

Ps 78

Day 17

"We give thanks to you, O God; we give thanks; your name is near. People tell of your wondrous deeds" (75:1).

Psalm 73
Plea for Relief from Oppressors

O my all-sufficient God,
 You know my heart's desire,
Be this single thing bestowed,
 I nothing else require,
Nothing else in earth or skies,
No quality so good or true,
 Heaven itself could not suffice:
 I seek not yours, but you.

Psalm 74
Prayer for Help in Time of National Humiliation

O Lord from heaven, on earth bestowed,
 Your goodness makes our blessings sure:
Your strength sustains us with our food,
 Your grace does in the medicine cure,
Whatever through your means you do,
Our help is all derived from you.

Psalm 76

Israel's God—Judge of All the Earth

I vow, resolve, and promise Lord,
  Through your sufficient grace
To avoid the thing by you abhorred,
  And walk in all your ways:
Depending in your blood applied,
  Armed with your Spirit's power,
My bosom-sin I lay aside,
  And never act it more.

Psalm 77

God's Mighty Deeds Recalled

1. Have mercy, Lord, your wrath remove,
  Nor let your judgments weigh me down,
I cannot live without your love,
  I cannot stand beneath your frown.

7. Forever is your mercy gone,
  Your truth, and faithfulness, and love?
Does angry justice rule alone?
  Have I no advocate above?

Psalm 78

God's Goodness and Israel's Ingratitude

1. Lord, I confess your judgments just,
If left to my own heart's desires,
I follow every brutal lust,
And do whate'er the flesh requires,
And led by Satan at his will,
The measure of my sin fulfil.

2. But for your endless mercy's sake,
Appear my Advocate with God,
The brand out of the burning take,
The brand extinguish with your blood,
Fountain of all our needful cures,
Now swallow up my will in yours.

On one of his excursions into Wales Wesley encountered violence as never before. One man who had been incensed by his preaching attacked him viciously. Charles's friend, Felix Farley, wrested a sword from his hand. Wesley told him calmly that it was his steadfast principle to return good for evil. He asked his friends to release him, assured him of his good wishes, put his arm around him, and invited him to walk by the waterside. Wesley's defenders stood aghast. Wesley simply befriended him and later wrote in his journal: "Human wrath serves only to praise you, when you bind the last bit of your wrath around you" (Psalm 76:10).

Questions for Thought or Discussion

The final line of Wesley's paraphrase of Psalm 73 is telling: "I seek not yours, but you." How has sheltering in the Psalms enhanced your "personal" relationship with God?

"I vow, resolve, and promise Lord" implies an extremely profound commitment. What have you promised to do or to avoid in order to walk God's way, and how is it going?

Psalms 77 and 78 both emphasize human impotency with regard to following God's path. In what areas of your life do you find it necessary to lean on God more fully?

Prayer & Blessing

"Whom have I in heaven but you? And there is nothing on earth that I desire other than you. My flesh and my heart may fail, but God is the strength of my heart and my portion forever" (73:25-26).

Day 18

Centering Prayer

"Restore us, O Most God of hosts; let your face shine, that we may be saved" (80:19).

Psalm 79

Plea for Mercy for Jerusalem

5. Save us by grace through faith alone,
   A faith you must yourself impart,
A faith that would by works be shown,
   A faith that purifies the heart.

6. A faith that does the mountains move,
   A faith that shows our sins forgiven,
A faith that sweetly works by love,
   And justifies our claim to heaven.

Psalm 80

Prayer for Israel's Restoration

26. Revive, O God of power, revive
   Your work in our conflicted days,
O let us by your mercy live,
   And all our lives shall speak your praise.

27. Turn us again, O Lord, and show
   The brightness of your lovely face,
So shall we all be saints below,
   And saved, and perfected in grace.

Psalm 81

God's Appeal to Stubborn Israel

Sing we merrily to God,
 We the creatures of God's grace,
We the purchase of God's blood
 Only live to sing and praise,
Make we then a cheerful noise,
 Every child of Adam joined
Share the universal joys,
 Shout the friend of humankind.

Psalm 83

Prayer for Judgment on Israel's Foes

1 The Lord our God is only One,
 One is Jehovah the most high:
Jehovah is God's name alone,
 Who made and fills both earth and sky:
Jehovah is the Savior's name;
 Jehovah is the Spirit's too:
And Three essentially the same
 Is the eternal God and true.

WESLEY TESTIMONY

The strongest opposition to the Wesleyan revival often came from inside the church. This pained Charles Wesley deeply. He sought renewal and renovation, not confrontation. On November 16, 1740 he preached from John 8, focusing on the contention between Jesus and the Pharisees. His prayed, "Help us, O God of our salvation, for the glory of your name; deliver us, and forgive our sins, for your name's sake" (Psalm 79:9). He confided to his journal: "I began abruptly with the opposers, and defied them in the name of the Lord Jesus. The Spirit of power was with me. But I soon perceived him as the Spirit of love."

Questions for Thought or Discussion

Wesley's paraphrase of Psalm 79 provides a string of one-line definitions of faith. Which of these dimensions of faith relates most closely to you in your life?

If "revival" means "restoration," what are those aspects of your life that God needs to revive?

"Jehovah" is the Latinization of the Hebrew word for God, YHWH. Think of all the names of God you can remember from scripture. Which means the most to you, and why?

Prayer & Blessing

"I am the Most High your God, who brought you up out of the land of Egypt.
Open your mouth wide and I will fill it" (81:10).

Day 19

Centering Psalm

> *"How lovely is your dwelling place,*
> *O God of hosts" (84:1)!*

Psalm 84
The Joy of Worship in the Temple

1. How lovely is your dwelling place,
O Lord of mercy and of grace,
    Your place of rest a house of prayer;
My soul outflies the angel-choir,
And faints o're-powered with strong desire,
    To meet your special presence there.

My heart and flesh cry out for God;
There would I fix my soul's abode,
    As birds that in your altars nest;
There would I all my young ones bring,
An offering to my God and King,
    And in your courts forever rest.

Psalm 85
Prayer for the Restoration of God's Favor

4. The tokens of your favor show,
    Now, Savior, now the grace impart,
And let us your salvation know,
    Forgiveness written on our heart.
My soul pursues the Spirit's prayer,
    I listen for the sacred sign,

The Lord shall soon a word declare,
　　And answer me in peace divine.
7. Truth shall spring up, (the truth of grace),
　　From earthly souls through Christ forgiven,
While God reveals a smiling face,
　　And righteousness looks down from heaven.
The Lord from all our sins shall save;
　　Our souls God's love delights to bless
Shall thrive, and flourish fair, and have
　　Their fruit to perfect holiness.

Psalm 86

Supplication for Help against Enemies

1. Bow down, O Lord, your gracious ear,
Your poor and needy servant hear;
　　My soul is all your own:
Preserve me, O my God, and save,
Faith in your mighty power I have,
　　I trust in you alone.

8. Teach me, O Lord, your perfect way,
My simple heart shall then obey,
　　With filial fear adore,
Then all my heart your name shall bless,
And praise, and sing, and never cease,
　　And love you ever more.

Psalm 88

Prayer for Help in Despondency

3. Ah faith in your redeeming blood
　　If you concede to give,

My soul shall quit this dark abode,
　　The moment I believe;
The chains of sin fall off my heart,
　　And freed by your own love,
I'll wait till you the joy impart,
　　And praise your name above.

Psalm 89

God's Covenant with David

My Lord, omnipotent to save,
　　Your glory and your life you gave
　　To claim my soul for good:
Your covenant grace to all extends,
Your love for all, it never ends,
　　And brings us all to God.

WESLEY TESTIMONY

On October 29, 1756 Charles Wesley wrote: "Nothing but grace can keep our children, after our departure, from running into a thousand sects, a thousand errors. Grace exercised, kept up, and increased in the use of all the means, especially family and public prayer, and Sacrament, will keep them steady. Let us labor while we continue here to ground and guide them up in the Scriptures and all the ordinances. . . . Should I live to see you again, I trust you will assure me, there is not a member of all your Societies but reads the Scripture daily, uses private prayer, joins in family and public worship, and communicates constantly."

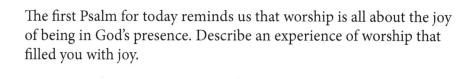

Questions for Thought or Discussion

The first Psalm for today reminds us that worship is all about the joy of being in God's presence. Describe an experience of worship that filled you with joy.

In Kenya we sang a chorus based on Psalm 86:8: "There is none like you among the gods, O Lord." It included spontaneous verses that gave voice to God's surpassing greatness. What verses about the unique qualities of our God would you sing?

"Covenant" is a pervasive theme throughout scripture. What are all the images you associate with covenant, and how do they apply to your life?

Prayer & Blessing

"You said, 'I have made a cov-
enant with my chosen one,
I have sworn to my servant
David: 'I will establish your
descendants forever,
and build your throne for all
generations'" (89:3-4).

Book Four: **Psalms 90-106**

"From everlasting to everlasting you are God"

Ps 90

Day 20

"You who live in the shelter of the Most High,
who abide in the shadow of the Almighty, will say to God,
"My refuge and my fortress; my God,
in whom I trust" (91:1-2).

Psalm 90

God's Eternity and Human Frailty

1. You, Lord, our dwelling-place have been,
Your faithful people rest within
    Your everlasting arms secure,
Them you have kept in ages past,
And still their guardian rock stands fast,
    Your mercies like yourself endure.

E'er at your word the mountains rose,
Or nature felt her earliest throes,
    Or all things out of nothing came,
You were from all eternity,
You are the God, and still shall be
    Through all eternity the same.

Psalm 91

Assurance of God's Protection

8. Charged by the sovereign King of kings
To guard, and keep the royal heir,
   The angels wrap you in their wings,
And in their hands securely bear,
Preserve your life, nor let you meet
   A stone to wound your sacred feet.

Psalm 93

The Majesty of God's Rule

2. Ancient of Days, your name
    And essence is I AM,
You, O Lord, and you alone
    Made whatever is to be,
Stood your everlasting throne
    Stands to all eternity.

5. Your statutes, Lord, are sure,
    And as yourself endure,
Your eternal house above
    Holy souls alone can view,
Fitted here by perfect love
    There to reign enthroned with you.

Psalm 94

God the Avenger of the Righteous

1. Almighty God, to whom alone
   Avenging power belongs,
Hear your afflicted people groan,
   And vindicate their wrongs.
To vindicate the oppressed is yours,
   To do the injured right,
Your great prerogative endures,
   All evil to requite.

2. Show yourself now, arise, O Lord,
   Judge of the earth appear,
Render the proud their due reward,
   And stop their triumphs here.
How long shall evil here proceed,
   That stirs up cruel mistrust?
With bitterness and hate o'erspread,
   That trample on the just?

WESLEY TESTIMONY

Wesley embarked for England from Georgia in Autumn 1736. On October 28 the captain warned everyone of an approaching storm. The seas rose higher and higher until the storm broke on them at sunset in the late evening hours. When the long-awaited morning came, the storm was still in its full fury. It washed away all the sheep, half the hogs, and drowned almost all the fowl. It took all the effort of four men, pumping continuously, to keep the ship above water. Wesley prayed for power to pray, for faith in Jesus, continually repeating his name, until the storm calmed and he knew he lived in the shelter of the Most High (Psalm 91:1).

Questions for Thought or Discussion:

How does Wesley describe God in his opening stanza of Psalm 90?

In the paraphrase of Psalm 93, Wesley uses the language of the great "I AM." What does this language indicate to you about the nature and essence of God?

Where do you see God at work in the world today to vindicate justice and the afflicted?

Prayer & Blessing

*"Those who love me, I will
deliver; I will protect those
who know my name.
When they call to me, I will
answer them; I will be
with them in trouble, I will
rescue them and honor them"*
(91:14-15).

Day 21

Centering Psalm

> *"Make a joyful noise to God, all the earth.*
> *Worship God with gladness; come into God's*
> *presence with singing" (100:1-2).*

Psalm 97
The Glory of God's Reign

1.The Lord unrivaled reigns
    And regal power maintains:
Earth your awesome monarch bless,
    Own with joy God's happy sway,
Ah let every child confess,
    All exult their God to obey.

8.The light of grace is sown
    For every simple one;
Reap the fruits of joy and peace,
    Righteous souls, the promise prove,
Thank God for this giftedness,
    Glory in God's perfect love.

Psalm 98
Praise of the Judge of the World

1. Sing we to our conquering Lord
    A new triumphant song,
Joyfully God's deeds record,
    And with a thankful tongue:
Wonders God's right-hand has wrought,

(Still God's outstretched arm we see)
God alone the fight has fought,
　　And got the victory.

6. Oceans roar with all your waves
　　In honor of God's name:
God who all creation saves
　　Does all their homage claim,
Clap your hands O floods and hills,
　　Joyful all God's praise rehearse,
Praise God, till God's glory fills
　　The vocal universe.

Psalm 99

Praise to God for God's Holiness

1.My God, you do forgive,
　　You do your child reprove;
　　And lo, my pardon I receive
With your redeeming love,
　　Accept my punishment
　　With trust in all you do,
My journey all-way through.

Psalm 100

All Lands Summoned to Praise God

1. O child of God, lift up your voice,
All nations of the earth rejoice,
　　In God rejoice with one accord,
Bow all your hearts before God's face,
Adore God for creating grace,
　　And shout, and sing to Christ the Lord.

2. Know, that the Lord is God alone,
God made, and claims us for God's own,
   God's creatures, for Godself designed,
We are the sheep of Israel's fold,
The flock God has redeemed of old,
   God's people, now is humankind.

3. O enter then God's courts with praise,
Receive the channels of God's grace,
   With joyful thanks your God proclaim:
Give God the glory for great love,
And praise God, like the hosts above,
   And bless God's all-redeeming name.

4. Praise God, the faithful Lord and good;
God's mercy has for ages stood,
   God's mercy stands forever sure,
God's steadfast truth shall never fail,
God's word and oath unchangeable
   Through all eternity endure

WESLEY TESTIMONY

On Thursday, August 23, 1744, Charles and his brother, John, returned together to Oxford. They spent some time reminiscing about their time in the "Holy Club." Charles preached to a large gathering of people who filled the inn and garden where they were staying. Many seemed struck and even astonished by their singing. Charles referenced Colossians 3:16 in his journal: "Let the Word of Christ, rich as it is, dwell in you. Instruct and admonish one another wisely. Sing gratefully to God from your hearts in psalms, hymns and songs of the Spirit." He concluded, "O that all the world had a taste for our diversion"—to sing a new song.

Questions for Thought or Discussion

In Psalm 97 Wesley celebrates the gifts, the fruits of joy and peace. What has brought you joy and filled you with peace these days?

The Psalmist frequently describes the ways in which God connects with everything in the universe. Wesley's hymn on Psalm 98 describes "the vocal universe." What are the sounds of nature that bring you peace and contentment?

The statement, "Enter God's gates with thanksgiving, and God's courts with praise," is one of the most famous in the Psalter. Reflect on an experience of thanksgiving and praise you experienced in worship and how it moved you?

Prayer & Blessing

"Light dawns for the righteous, and joy for the upright in heart" (97:11).

Day 22

"Bless God, O my soul, and all that is within me,
bless God's holy name" (103:1).

Psalm 101

A Sovereign's Pledge of Integrity and Justice

1. When will you come unto me
    And bid my troubles cease,
After your mind renew me
    In truth and righteousness?
I want the heavenly Giver
    More than the gifts divine:
Come to a weak believer,
    My Lord, forever mine.

Psalm 102

Prayer to the Eternal Ruler for Help

1. Hear, O Lord, my bitter cry,
    Regard my sad complaint,
Do not now your help deny
    When most your help I want;
Hide not now your face from me,
Your ear in tender mercy bow,
    Hearken, to my heartfelt plea,
    Relieve, relieve me now.

2. All my days, like smoke expire
    In vanity and sin,

Sin as a consuming fire
    I find shut up within:
Droops my heart, as grass cut down,
No more my nature's wants I heed,
    Groaning underneath your frown,
        My tears are all my bread.

Psalm 103

Thanksgiving for God's Goodness

1. Praise the Lord, my thankful soul,
    God let all within me praise!
God again has made me whole,
    God has lengthened out my days.

2. Gracious, merciful, and kind,
    God my thankful soul proclaim,
Bear God's benefits in mind,
    Love, and bless God's hallowed name.

Psalm 104

God the Creator and Provider

1. Author of every work divine,
You, who through both creations shine,
    The God of nature and of grace,
Your glorious steps in all we view,
And wisdom celebrate in you,
    And power, and majesty, and praise.

Psalm 106

A Confession of Sin of Israel's Sins

1. Your mercy, Lord, is better
    Than life and all below:
Visit your fallen creature
    That I your love may know,
The Three-One's habitation,
    Your Spirit's constant home,
O come with your salvation,
    With all the Godhead come.

WESLEY TESTIMONY

In the days immediately prior to Charles
Wesley's conversion, he filled his journal
with entries like, "Waked without Christ" and
"weary, faithless, and heartless." He felt so
heavy that he confesses being unable even
to pray. But his desire for God never left him,
and he always reports finding comfort in the
Word and in reading prayers when he could
not formulate his own. He found particular
comfort in the prayer of David: "Do not hide
your face from me in the day of my distress.
Incline your ear to me; answer me speedily
in the day when I call" (Psalm 102:2). God
opened his eyes increasingly to the promise
of redemption.

Questions for Thought or Discussion

"I want the heavenly Giver / More than the gifts divine." Do you seek God more than God's gifts? How might you embrace the Giver of every good gift more fully?

"Relieve, relieve me now" is a heartfelt cry. When and why has this been your prayer?

The Psalms celebrate God's grace in creation and in recreation. What lessons about our life with God do we learn from both expressions of grace?

Prayer & Blessing

"Bless God, O my soul, and do not forget all God's benefits—who forgives all your iniquity, who heals all your diseases, who redeems your life from the Pit, who crowns you with steadfast love and mercy, who satisfies you with good as long as you live so that your youth is renewed like the eagle's" (103:2-5).

Book Five: **Psalms 107-150**

"God
stands
at the right
hand
of the
needy"

Ps 109

Day 23

Centering Psalm

*"God gives the childless woman a home, making her
the joyous mother of children" (113:9).*

Psalm 107

Thanksgiving for Deliverance from Many Troubles

10. Dreadful in power, as rich in grace
God frowns, and changes nature's face,
    Where sinners load the guilty land,
God looks their springs and rivers dry,
Their fertile fields as deserts lie
    Accursed, and turned to barren sand.

God smiles, and makes the desert smile,
Blesses your dry unfruitful soil,
    With living streams the land supplies,
The waste is clothed with sudden green,
And herbs, and flowers, and fruits are seen
    Throughout the rising paradise.

Psalm 110

Assurance of Victory for God's Priest-Ruler

7. Come now, and claim me for your own,
    Savior, your right assert,
Come, gracious Lord, set up your throne,
    And reign within my heart.

15. To you shall heaven and earth submit,

And every foe shall fall,
Till death expires beneath your feet,
And God is all in all!

Psalm 111

Praise for God's Wonderful Works

Your covenant this, that I shall know
    The love that you now have for me,
Shall feel God's blood and Spirit flow
    And in your grace be cleansed and free,
Ne'er from my Parent's arms remove,
Loved with an everlasting love.

Psalm 113

God the Helper of the Needy

3. Though it's beneath God's state to view
In highest heavens what angels do,
    Yet God to earth dispenses care:
God lifts the needy from their hell,
Advancing them in courts to dwell,
    Companions of the greatest there.

Psalm 114

God's Wonders at the Exodus

1. When Israel out of Egypt came,
    And left the proud oppressor's land,
Conducted by the great I AM,
    Safe in the hollow of God's hand;
The Lord in Israel reigned alone,
And Judah was God's favorite throne.

2. The sea beheld God's power, and fled,
      Dis-parted by the wondrous rod,
Jordan ran backward to its head,
      And Sinai felt the incumbent God,
The mountains skipped like frightened rams,
The hills leaped after them as lambs.

WESLEY TESTIMONY

On the day following his conversion, Wesley confided to his journal: "Monday, May 22, 1738. Under his protection I waked next morning and rejoiced in reading Psalm 107, so nobly describing what God had done for my soul. "Give thanks for God's goodness; God's love endures forever!" Let these be the words of God's redeemed, those redeemed from the oppressor's clutches" (verses 1-2). I fell asleep again and waked out of a dream that I was fighting with two devils—had one under my feet; the other faced me some time, but faded, and sunk, and vanished away, upon my telling him I belonged to Christ."

Questions for Thought or Discussion

God smiles, and everything changes according to Psalm 109. How has God's smile rocked your world?

Psalm 113:7 celebrates how God "raises the poor from the dust, and lifts the needy from the ash heap." How can you more fully engage with God in this work?

The Psalms rehearse the "mighty acts of God" through which God demonstrates love and care. Psalm 114 employs the primary image of liberation. What is the most significant way in which God has liberated you?

Prayer & Blessing

"Let them thank God for God's steadfast love, for the wonderful works to humankind.
For God satisfies the thirsty, and fills the hungry with good things" (107:8-9)

Day 24

> *O give thanks to God, for God is good; God's steadfast love endures forever" (118:1)!*

Psalm 116

Thanksgiving for Recovery from Illness

1. The Lord saves through the gift of grace,
    And ransoms the oppressed,
My dear redeeming Lord I praise,
    And in God's love I rest.
Since God a pitying ear did give,
    And heard me when I prayed,
I'll call upon God while I live,
    And never doubt God's aid.

4. Then, O my soul be never more
    With anxious thoughts distressed,
Return, for all the storm is o're,
    To your eternal rest.
On me the riches of God's grace
    My Savior has bestowed,
And lo! I see God's smiling face
    And bless my God, my God.

Psalm 117

Universal Call to Worship

1. O nations, who the globe divide,
So many nations scattered wide,

To God your grateful voices raise:
To all God's boundless mercies shown,
God's truth to endless ages known
    Require our endless love and praise.

2. To God who reigns enthroned on high,
To God's dear Son who deigned to die,
    Our guilt and errors to remove;
To that blessed Spirit who grace imparts,
Who rules in all believing hearts
    Be ceaseless glory, praise, and love.

Psalm 118

A Song of Victory

1. All glory to our gracious Lord;
God's love be by the church adored.
    God's love eternally the same:
God's love let thankful hearts confess,
God's free and everlasting grace
    Let all that fear the Lord proclaim.

In trouble, on the Lord I cried,
And felt the pardoning word applied;
    God answered me in peace and power,
God plucked my soul out of the net,
In a large place of safety set,
    And bade me go, and sin no more.

6. The voice of joy, and love, and praise,
And thanks for God's redeeming grace
    Among the justified is found:
With songs that rival those above,

With shouts proclaiming Jesus' love,
　　Both day and night their tents resound.

The Lord's right hand has wonders wrought,
Above the reach of human thought,
　　The Lord's right hand exalted is;
We see it still stretched out to save,
The power of God in Christ we have,
　　And Jesus is the Prince of Peace.

WESLEY TESTIMONY

On July 24, 1743 Wesley once again encountered an angry mob. As he described the circumstances, he said that he passed by an unruly crowd and then walked on slowly with all the rabble behind him. The Lord, as he recalled, hid him in the palm of God's hand. But when the mob continued to pursue him, he simply stood before them and looked them squarely in the face without saying a word. They pulled off their hats and cowered away. Quoting Psalm 118:16, Charles said that the Lord was pre-eminent and won the victory. The Methodist Society gathered and their hearts danced for joy. They praised God with one of Charles's hymns.

Questions for Thought or Discussion

The Psalms for this day reflect the Psalmists affirmation of the central place of grace in our relationship to God. What does salvation by grace mean to you?

The final line from Psalm 116 quoted above exclaims "my God, my God." What does it mean to you to use this kind of language about God?

Psalm 118 could be described as an exuberant song of victory. How has God's victory in your life put a song in your heart?

Prayer & Blessing

"Praise God, all you nations!
Extol God, all you peoples!
For great is God's steadfast
love toward us,
and the faithfulness of God
endures forever. Hallelujah"
(117)!

Day 25

Centering Psalm

"Oh, how I love your law!
It is my meditation all day long" (119:97).

Psalm 119

The Glories of God's Law

1.

1. Blessed are the pure in heart,
    Those who never disobey,
Never from their Lord depart,
    Never leave God's perfect way:
From all sin entirely freed
    Here they walk with God above,
Born again, and saints indeed,
    Fully perfected in love.

2.

4. In the records of your love
    I have found a mine of joy,
All my treasure is above,
    While your words my thoughts employ.
Still to search your word of grace,
    This is all I seek to do,
Still to know your pleasant ways,
    Still to love, and walk in you.

3.

1. Your unworthy servant, Lord,
    With abundant grace receive,

That I may fulfil your Word,
    Bid me by your mercy live:
Open now my inward eyes,
    From the Book the veil remove,
That I may discern the prize,
    The high prize of perfect love.

5.

1. Teach me, Lord, the perfect way,
    Me who on your love depend,
Then I in your laws shall stay,
    I shall keep them to the end.
Wisdom from above impart,
    Taught according to your will,
I shall then with all my heart
    All your kind commands fulfil.

6.

4. You, O Lord, I still obey
    You with vast delight pursue,
Walking in your pleasant way,
    Glad your dear commands to do;
Lo! for this I lift my hands,
    With a solemn oath approve,
All your merciful commands,
    All your gracious Law of Love.

14.

1. Lord, your Word's unerring light,
    As a lamp my path does show,
Guides my steady feet aright;
    All who walk this path do know.
I have sworn to do your will;
    Through your all-sufficient

Grace I shall all my vows fulfil,
    Shall fulfil all righteousness.

18.
1. Sovereign everlasting Lord,
    You are perfect righteousness:
Pure is your unerring Word,
    Upright are your high decrees:
Righteous all your statutes are,
    You the merciful they prove,
You the faithful they declare,
    Full of truth and full of love.

22,
2. Joyful at your Word, as one
    That has found a precious store,
There I search for bliss unknown
    Every other quest give o're.
Hating all deceitful ways
    I your Law with joy approve,
Offer you continual praise,
    Bless you for your faithful love.

WESLEY TESTIMONY

Charles Wesley met Jesus at the Lord's Supper frequently. Because of this, he described the sacrament as a means of grace. He also believed that, at the Communion table, God teaches us supremely about the law—the law of love. On January 13, 1745 he found himself in much distress at the altar. He opened his Bible and his eyes fell to Psalm 119:71: "It was good for me to have been afflicted, because through it I learned your statutes." He describes his heart being full of prayer. "At last I broke out into tears and strong cries," he testifies, "and all with me. It was indeed a glorious time of visitation."

Questions for Thought or Discussion

Today's Psalm is the longest in the Bible—176 verses in 22 sections set out as an acrostic of the Hebrew alphabet. The Psalmist delights in and lives by God's Law. What does it mean to you to "walk in the Law."

Wesley talks about both searching and knowing God's Law. Describe the ways in which you search so as to know God's way.

In these several stanzas, Wesley draws a close connection between God's Law and God's Love. In your view, what part does the Law play in perfecting you in love?

Prayer & Blessing

"Your statutes have been my songs wherever I make my home. I remember your name in the night, O Most High, and keep your law. This blessing has fallen to me, for I have kept your precepts" (119:54-56).

Day 26

Centering Psalm

*"I lift up my eyes to the hills—from where will my help come?
My help comes from God, who made heaven and earth"*

(121:1-2).

Psalm 120

Prayer for Deliverance from Slanderers

1. To God in trouble I applied,
    And God redressed my wrong;
Save me from lying lips, I cried,
    And a deceitful tongue.

Psalm 121

Assurance of God's Protection

1 To the hills I lift my eyes
    The everlasting hills,
Streaming thence in fresh supplies,
    My soul the Spirit feels:
Will the Spirit help afford?
    Help, while yet I ask, is given:
God comes down: the God and Lord
    That made both earth and heaven.

Psalm 122

Song of Praise and Prayer for Jerusalem

1 O how overjoyed was I,
When the solemn hour drew nigh!

Summoned to the house of prayer
Flew my soul to worship there.

My brothers and my sisters said,
Let us go with holy speed;
Let us haste with one accord
To the temple of our Lord.

Psalm 123

Supplication for Mercy

4. Harassed and hated for your cause,
    Your gracious favor we implore;
Help us now endure the cross,
    Till all their tyranny is o'er,
Till Christ with our reward comes down
And every sufferer wears a crown.

Psalm 124

Thanksgiving for Israel's Deliverance

2. Had not the Lord (we now may cry)
    Appeared God's people to sustain,
The threatening floods that dashed the sky,
    Had whirled us down to hell again;
O'erwhelmed us in the gulf beneath,
And plunged our souls in endless death.

3. But God has quelled their angry pride,
    And kept us in our evil hour,
God's name be blessed and glorified,
    God has not left us to their power,
God's word restrained their lawless will,
And bade the raging sea be still.

Psalm 125

The Security of God's People

2. As round Jerusalem
     The hilly bulwarks rise,
So God protects and covers them
     From all their enemies:
     On every side God stands,
     And for all Israel cares,
And safe in God's almighty hands
     Their souls forever bears.

Psalm 126

A Harvest of Joy

7. Those who bear their fears,
     And wet their path with tears,
Doubtless shall they soon return,
     Bring their sheaves with vast increase,
Fully of the Spirit born,
     Perfected in holiness.

WESLEY TESTIMONY

Wesley loved the church. On September 24, 1756 he encountered a group of Methodists who were eager to separate from the Church of England. They were determined to manage their own spiritual lives. They were tired of priests and what they considered to be meaningless traditions. Charles simply advised them all to go to church. Later he preached as vigorously as he could on the significance of the community of faith, telling them directly that there was no salvation outside the company of God's faithful people. Afterward they were all of one mind and heart and even glad when Wesley said, "Let us go into the house of the Lord" (Psalm 122:1).

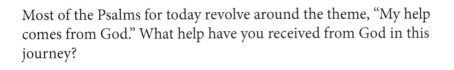

Questions for Thought or Discussion

Most of the Psalms for today revolve around the theme, "My help comes from God." What help have you received from God in this journey?

What robs you of your sense of security? Who are the people to whom you can turn when you feel insecure?

The phrase "bringing in their sheaves" comes from Psalm 126. It celebrates the abundant harvest of joy we have in God. What are the elements of that harvest for you?

Blessing

"May those who sow in tears
reap with shouts of joy.
Those who go out weeping,
bearing the seed for sowing,
shall come home with shouts
of joy, carrying their sheaves"
(126:5-6).

Day 27

*"Unless God builds the house,
those who build it labor in vain" (127:1).*

Psalm 127

God's Blessings in the Home

1 Except the house Jehovah raise,
    Fruitless is all the builder's care,
Except Jehovah guard the place,
    In vain the watch is stationed there,
Nothing without God's hand is done,
To make and keep are God's alone.

Psalm 128

The Happy Home of the Faithful

7. The children of your faith and prayer,
    Your joyful eyes shall see,
Shall see the prosperous church, and share
    In her prosperity.

9. Filled with abiding peace divine,
    With Israel's blessing blessed,
You then the church above shall join,
    And gain your heavenly rest.

Psalm 129

Prayer for the Downfall of Israel's Enemies

3 The Lord, the righteous Lord, and true,
    Turned our captivity again,
The cords of wickedness broke through,
    And burst the dire oppressor's chain:
And still who Zion hate shall fly,
And stumble, and forever die.

Psalm 130

Waiting for Divine Redemption

1. Out of the deeps to you, O Lord!
    I make my mournful cry;
Incline your ear unto my voice,
    Your ready help apply.

3. I wait for God, my soul does wait,
    And in God's word I trust:
That word God surely shall fulfil,
    And raise me from the dust.

Psalm 131

Song of Quiet Trust

1. Lord, if you the grace impart,
Poor in spirit, meek in heart,
I shall as my Master be
Rooted in humility.

Psalm 132

The Eternal Dwelling of God in Zion

3. Arise, O Lord, into your rest,
    You, and your ark of perfect power,
God over all, forever blessed,
    You, Jesus, let our hearts adore.
Your priests be clothed with righteousness,
    Your praise their happy lives employ,
The saints in you their all possess,
    And shout your children all for joy.

Psalm 133

The Blessedness of Unity

1. Behold how good a thing
    It is to dwell in peace,
How pleasing to our King
    This fruit of righteousness,
When children of the Lord agree;
Who know the joy of unity!

Psalm 134

Praise in the Night

1. Ye servants of God, whose diligent care
Is ever employed in watching and prayer,
With praises unceasing your Jesus proclaim,
Rejoicing and blessing his excellent name.

WESLEY TESTIMONY

In late August 1744 the Holy Spirit was poured out on the Methodist community in and around Bristol. "Great was the cry after Jesus," Wesley testifies. "Many a soul fell at his feet and said, 'Lord, help me.'" He celebrated Communion with a Methodist woman at death's door and said that all those present were partakers of her joy. He spent an hour in prayerful intercession for his beloved Church, returning to the words of Psalm 133:1 time and time again and celebrating how good a thing it is to dwell together in unity. He felt the spirit of Jesus when he met with the Society; tears and rejoicing bore witness to his presence.

Questions for Thought or Discussion

Often we cry out to God "from the depths." What is the deep out of which you cry today?

Psalm 131 emphasizes the importance of humility in life. What are the practices in which you engage to cultivate a humble spirit?

Psalm 133 reads: "How very good and pleasant it is when kindred live together in unity!" What can you do to be a person who seeks reconciliation and unity today?

Blessing

"Blessed is everyone who reveres God, who walks in God's ways.
You shall eat the fruit of the labor of your hands;
you shall be happy, and it shall go well with you.
Thus shall the one be blessed who reveres God" (128:1-2, 4)

Day 28

"O God, you have searched me and known me" (139:1).

Psalm 135

Praise for God's Goodness and Might

2. Jesus, you have the faith bestowed
    In which to you I pray,
The barrier to my quest for good
    For ever take away;
The stubborn pulse, the cause within,
    The stumbling-block remove,
And form my soul averse from sin,
    And mold me into love.

Psalm 136

God's Work in Creation and in History

1. Full of great, unbounded grace,
Jesus my eye of faith surveys!
Jesus, whate'er you are is mine,
Fountain of excellence divine!
Your goodness is for all to see,
Good in yourself, and good to me.

2. Your nature does itself impart
To every humble longing heart;
And all that after you aspire
Shall gain with you their whole desire,
United to their source above,
Lost in a boundless sea of love.

Psalm 137

Lament over the Destruction of Jerusalem

1 Fast by the Babylonish tide,
(The tide our sorrows made o'erflow)
We dropped our weary limbs, and cried
In deep distress at Zion's woe,
Her we bewailed in speechless groans
In bondage with her captive sons.

2 Our harps, no longer vocal now,
We cast aside untuned, unstrung,
Forgot them pendant on the bough;
Let lesser sorrows find a tongue.
Silent we sat, and scorned relief,
In all the majesty of grief.

3 In vain our haughty lords required
A song of Zion's sacred strain,
"Sing us a song your God inspired."
How shall our souls exult in pain,
How shall the mournful exiles sing,
While bond-slaves to a foreign king?

4 Jerusalem dear hallowed name,
You if I ever less desire,
If less distressed for you I am,
Let my right hand forget its lyre,
All its harmonious strains forgo,
When heedless of a mother's woe.

Psalm 138

Thanksgiving and Praise

1. All thanks and all praise
   To you will I give,
O Lord, by whose grace
   Accepted I live:
My heart shall adore,
   While seeking your face,
My spirit shall soar,
   With thanks and with praise.

Psalm 139

The Inescapable God

1. Whither shall a creature run?
   From Jehovah's Spirit fly?
How Jehovah's presence shun,
   Screened from God's all-seeing eye?
Holy Ghost, before your face,
   Where shall I myself conceal?
You are God in every place,
God incomprehensible.

Charles Wesley married Sally Gwynne on April 8, 1749. He always believed that his relationship with Sally shaped him into a more loving person. Just like God, she knew him genuinely and loved him deeply. He connected these two loves of his life in his own heart. "Not a cloud was to be seen from morning till night," he testifies. "I rose at four, spent three hours and an half in prayer, or singing, with my brother, with Sally, with Becky. At eight I led MY SALLY to church. Mr. Gwynne gave her to me (under God). My brother joined our hands. It was a most solemn season of love! Never had I more of the divine presence at the Sacrament."

Questions for Thought or Discussion

Charles Wesley's lyrical paraphrase of Psalm 135 includes the image of being molded into love. How has God, like a potter, been molding you into a more loving person?

The Psalmist's lament over Jerusalem (emptiness) is sandwiched between two songs that celebrate the fullest possible connection with God, peace, and love. How do you make sense of this juxtaposition?

One of my spiritual mentors told me that if I prayed Psalm 139 every day for a month, it would change my life. What are some of the life-changing elements of this song for you?

Blessing

"Though I walk in the midst of trouble, you preserve me against the wrath of my enemies; you stretch out your hand, and your right hand delivers me.
God will fulfill God's purpose for me; your steadfast love, O God, endures forever"
(138:7-8).

Day 29

Centering Psalm

"When my spirit is faint, you know my way" (142:3).

Psalm 140

Prayer for Deliverance from Enemies

5. Sure I am, divinely sure,
   Help I have not asked in vain,
God shall vindicate the poor,
   God shall soon my cause maintain;
On the Lord I dare rely,
Poor, and weak, and helpless I!

Psalm 141

Prayer for Preservation from Evil

My God, forsake me not at last,
Nor into utter darkness cast
   A soul that for you gasps:
When I my pilgrimage have borne,
I humbly trust, you will return,
   My God that my soul grasps.

Psalm 142

Prayer for Deliverance from Persecutors

5. My soul out of the dungeon bring,
That I your conquering name may sing,
   Your saving grace proclaim,

That all your saints may praise your power,
Your all-sufficient grace adore,
  Your all-redeeming name.

Psalm 143
Prayer for Deliverance from Enemies

5. See, Lord, a dying sinner view,
    I still stretch out my hands to you,
Unwashed and unrenewed,
    As thirsts a barren land for showers,
My weary soul with all its powers
Gasps for the living God.

8. For refuge, Lord, to you I fly,
    On you alone for help rely,
For pardon, peace, and power:
    From all my foes, and sins release,
And teach me thus my Lord to please
And bid me sin no more.

Psalm 144
Prayer for National Deliverance and Security

Jesus, you are my Lord, my God,
    And happy in your love I am:
The bliss you have on me bestowed
    Remains in life and death the same;
The love to all your people given
Is present, and eternal heaven.

Psalm 145

The Greatness and the Goodness of God

You show that I may mercy claim:
    I bring no other plea;
Most modest of your works I am,
    And mercy found out me.

WESLEY TESTIMONY

On Wednesday, March 14, 1744, Wesley testified to God's protection when the Methodist
chapel at Leeds collapsed under the weight of
so many people during preaching. The rafters
simply broke off close to the main beam. But
Charles had shifted the congregation inside
to one end, just moments before, so that those
outside could hear him more clearly. A sick
woman in a room below had called the nurse
a minute before who carried her baby with
her to the opposite end of the building. All
three were unharmed. Charles escaped with
cuts and bruises. More than a hundred lay
with him among the injured, but not one life
was lost.

Questions for Thought or Discussion

Several of the Psalms today describe the child of God "gasping" for the One they love. Describe a time in your life when you too gasped for God and what it has meant to you.

The words of the Psalmist, "When my spirit is faint, you know my way" (142:3), may have inspired the prayer of Dietrich Bonhoeffer in prison, "I do not understand your ways, but you know the way for me." When have you felt this way?

Kyrie Eleison (Lord, have mercy) is one of the simplest and most profound prayers. How has the experience of God's mercy shaped your life?

Blessing

The eyes of all look to you, and you give them their food in due season.
You open your hand, satisfying the desire of every living thing (145:15-16).

Day 30

Centering Psalm

> *"Hallelujah! Praise God, O my soul! I will*
> *praise God as long as I live;*
> *I will sing praises to my God all my life long" (146:1-2)!*

Psalm 146
Praise for God's Help

1. My soul inspired with sacred love
     The Lord my God delight to praise,
   God's gifts I will for God improve,
     To God devote my happy days,
   To God my thanks and praises give,
   And only for God's glory live.

2. Long as my God shall lend me breath,
     My every pulse shall beat for God,
   And when my voice is lost in death,
     My powers shall up in love be caught;
   The glorious theme with vigor new
   Through all eternity pursue.

Psalm 147
Praise for God's Care for Jerusalem

   How pleasant a thing
   With thanksgiving to sing,
   As with joy from the vale we remove!
   But pleasanter still
   When we stand on the hill,
   And give thanks to our Savior above!

Psalm 149

Praise for God's Goodness to Israel

The God of love in saints delights
    Well pleaséd with the Son,
For whom true love to Christ unites
    They all with Christ are one.

Psalm 150

Praise for God's Surpassing Greatness

1. Praise the Lord who reigns above
    And keeps God's court below;
Praise the holy God of love
    And all God's greatness show;
Praise God for God's noble deeds,
    Praise God for God's matchless power;
God, from whom all good proceeds
    Let earth and heaven adore.

3. Celebrate the eternal God
    With harp and psaltery,
Timbrels soft and cymbals loud
    In God's high praise agree;
Praise with every tuneful string,
    All the reach of heavenly art,
All the powers of music bring,
    The music of the heart.

4. God, in whom they move, and live,
    Let every creature sing,
Glory to their Maker give,
    And homage to their King;
Hallowed be God's name beneath,
    As in heaven on earth adored:
Praise the Lord in every breath,
    Let all things praise the Lord!

WESLEY TESTIMONY

Charles Wesley engaged in an extended preaching tour throughout Cornwall in the summer of 1744. His account of Tuesday, July 31, typifies his experience of the Spirit throughout the course of those days. "Preached in the afternoon to a larger congregation than ever, and continued my discourse till night, from Luke 21:34. The Spirit of love was poured out abundantly, and great grace was upon all. Walked to the Society. Stood upon the hill, and sang, and prayed, and rejoiced with exceeding great joy. Concluded the day and month as I would wish to conclude my life. 'I will sing praises to my God all my life long'" (Psalm 146:2)!

Questions for Thought or Discussion

The conclusion of the Psalter (146-150) consists of one great act of praise. On this 30th day of sheltering with the Psalms, what songs of praise are you singing in your heart?

Charles Wesley's paraphrase of Psalm 150 continues to be sung today. As you read through this song again, what are the images of praise that strike you most?

What is the most significant thing you have learned from this experience of sheltering with the Psalms?

Blessing

Blessed are those whose help
is the God of Jacob,
whose hope is in the Most
High their God, who made
heaven and earth, the sea, and
all that is in them; who keeps
faith forever; who
executes justice for the
oppressed; who gives food to
the hungry; who sets the
prisoners free. God opens the
eyes of those who cannot see,
lifts up those who are bowed
down, and loves the righteous.
God watches over the stranger
and upholds the orphan and
the widow" (146:5-9).

SOURCES OF CHARLES WESLEY'S PSALM TEXTS

Source Abbreviations

CPH (1741)	John Wesley. *Collection of Psalms and Hymns*. London: Strahan, 1741.
CPH	John & Charles Wesley. *Collection of Psalms and Hymns*. 2nd edn., enlarged. London: Strahan, 1743
Earthquake	Charles Wesley. *Hymns occasioned by the Earthquake, March 8, 750. Part I*. London: Strahan, 1750.
HSP (1742)	John and Charles Wesley. *Hymns and Sacred Poems*. Bristol: Farley, 1742.
HSP (1749)	Charles Wesley. *Hymns and Sacred Poems*. 2 vols. Bristol: Farley, 1749. 2nd Bristol: Farley, 1755–56.
MS Psalms	Collection of Charles Wesley's manuscript Psalms hymns, Methodist Archive and Research Centre, The John Rylands Library, The University of Manchester.
MSSH (OT)	Collection of Charles Wesley's manuscript scripture hymns on texts of the Old Testament, Methodist Archive and Research Centre, The John Rylands Library, The University of Manchester.
SH	Charles Wesley. *Short Hymns on Select Passages of the Holy Scriptures*. 2 vols. Bristol: Farley, 1762.
Trinity	Charles Wesley. *Hymns on the Trinity*. Bristol: Pine, 1767.
Whitsunday	John and Charles Wesley. *Hymns of Petition and Thanksgiving for the Promise of the Father*. Bristol: Farley, 1746

Psalm 1	CPH, 1	Psalm 41	MS Psalms, 108-109
Psalm 2	CPH, 2-3	Psalm 42	MS Psalms, 110-12
Psalm 3	CPH, 4	Psalm 43	MS Psalms, 112-13
Psalm 4	CPH, 5	Psalm 44	MS Psalms, 117
Psalm 5	CPH, 7	Psalm 45	CPH, 74, 76-77
Psalm 6	CPH, 9	Psalm 46	Earthquake, 9-10
Psalm 7	MS Psalms, 11	Psalm 47	CPH, 77-78
Psalm 8	CPH, 66	Psalm 48	MS Psalms, 128
Psalm 9	MS Psalms, 15	Psalm 51	CPH, 12-14
Psalm 10	MS Psalms, 18	Psalm 52	MS Psalms, 140-41
Psalm 11	MS Psalms, 19	Psalm 54	MS Psalms, 142
Psalm 12	MS Psalms, 20-21	Psalm 55	MS Psalms, 144, 146
Psalm 13	CPH, 9	Psalm 56	CPH, 79-80
Psalm 14	MS Psalms, 23	Psalm 57	CPH, 80-81
Psalm 16	MS Psalms, 29	Psalm 58	MS Psalms, 152
Psalm 17	MS Psalms, 30	Psalm 59	MS Psalms, 156
Psalm 18	CPH, 68	Psalm 60	MS Psalms, 157
Psalm 19	MS Psalms, 40	Psalm 61	MS Psalms, 158-59
Psalm 20	MS Psalms, 43	Psalm 62	MS Psalms, 160-61
Psalm 21	MS Psalms, 44	Psalm 63	MS Psalms, 162-63
Psalm 22	MS Psalms, 46	Psalm 64	MS Psalms, 164-65
Psalm 23	MS Psalms, 50-51	Psalm 65	MS Psalms, 168
Psalm 24	CPH, 68, 70	Psalm 66	MS Psalms, 170-71
Psalm 25	MS Psalms, 54	Psalm 67	MS Psalms, 172-73
Psalm 26	MS Psalms, 58	Psalm 68	MS Psalms, 179
Psalm 27	MS Psalms, 58-59	Psalm 69	MS Psalms, 182-83
Psalm 28	MS Psalms, 62-63	Psalm 70	MS Psalms, 184
Psalm 29	MS Psalms, 65	Psalm 71	MS Psalms, 185, 187
Psalm 30	MS Psalms, 66, 68	Psalm 72	SH, 1:266
Psalm 31	MS Psalms, 68	Psalm 73	SH, 1:266
Psalm 32	CPH, 71	Psalm 74	SH, 1:267
Psalm 33	MS Psalms, 76-77	Psalm 76	MSSH (OT), 91
Psalm 34	MS Psalms, 80-81	Psalm 77	HSP (1742), 17-18
Psalm 35	MS Psalms, 88	Psalm 78	MSSH (OT), 93
Psalm 36	CPH, 72	Psalm 79	HSP (1749), 1:177
Psalm 37	MS Psalms, 95, 97	Psalm 80	CPH, 17
Psalm 38	MS Psalms, 99-100	Psalm 81	MSSH (OT), 60
Psalm 39	MS Psalms, 101-102	Psalm 83	Trinity, 72
Psalm 40	MS Psalms, 104-105	Psalm 84	MS Psalms, 212

Psalm 85	MS Psalms, 214-15		Psalm 126	CPH, 92
Psalm 86	MS Psalms, 216-17		Psalm 127	CPH, 92
Psalm 88	MSSH (OT), 62		Psalm 128	CPH, 94
Psalm 89	SH, 1:268		Psalm 129	CPH, 95
Psalm 90	MS Psalms, 222		Psalm 130	CPH (1741), 52-53
Psalm 91	MS Psalms, 226		Psalm 131	CPH, 95
Psalm 93	MS Psalms, 229-30		Psalm 132	CPH, 96
Psalm 94	MS Psalms, 231		Psalm 133	CPH, 97-98
Psalm 97	MS Psalms, 236, 237		Psalm 134	CPH, 99
Psalm 98	MS Psalms, 238, 239		Psalm 135	MSSH (OT), 78
Psalm 99	MSSH (OT), 66		Psalm 136	SH, 1:279
Psalm 100	MS Psalms, 241		Psalm 137	CPH, 21-22
Psalm 101	MSSH (OT), 67		Psalm 138	MS Psalms, 336
Psalm 102	MS Psalms, 243		Psalm 139	Trinity, 52, 53
Psalm 103	HSP (1742), 154		Psalm 140	MS Psalms, 342-43
Psalm 104	Whitsunday, 31		Psalm 141	SH, 1:280
Psalm 106	MSSH (OT), 70		Psalm 142	MS Psalms, 345-46
Psalm 107	MS Psalms, 262		Psalm 143	MS Psalms, 347-48
Psalm 110	HSP (1742), 90-91		Psalm 144	SH, 1:282
Psalm 111	SH, 1:272		Psalm 145	SH, 1:282
Psalm 113	MS Psalms, 270		Psalm 146	MS Psalms, 353
Psalm 114	CPH, 109		Psalm 147	SH, 1:283
Psalm 116	MS Psalms, 274-75		Psalm 149	SH, 1:283
Psalm 117	MS Psalms, 276-77		Psalm 150	CPH, 122
Psalm 118	MS Psalms, 278, 279-80			
Psalm 119.1	MS Psalms, 282			
Psalm 119.2	MS Psalms, 284			
Psalm 119.3	MS Psalms, 284			
Psalm 119.5	MS Psalms, 287			
Psalm 119.6	MS Psalms, 289			
Psalm 119.14	MS Psalms, 297			
Psalm 119.18	MS Psalms, 301			
Psalm 119.21	MS Psalms, 305			
Psalm 120	CPH, 85			
Psalm 121	CPH, 86			
Psalm 122	CPH, 87			
Psalm 123	CPH, 89			
Psalm 124	CPH, 89-90			
Psalm 125	CPH, 90			

ABOUT THE AUTHOR

PAUL W. CHILCOTE is currently serving in retirement as Director of the Centre for Global Wesleyan Theology at Wesley House, Cambridge. An award-winning author and retired Methodist historian and theologian, he is a frequent speaker and workshop leader in applied Wesleyan studies, particularly in the areas of theology, spirituality, and Christian discipleship. He served as the President of The Charles Wesley Society from 2003-2011. He has been a Benedictine oblate of Mt. Angel Abbey for nearly twenty-five years.

Made in the USA
Columbia, SC
15 February 2025

53877597R00113